THE
KINFOLK
TABLE

RECIPES *for* SMALL GATHERINGS

Nathan Williams
with Rebecca Parker Payne

Photographs by Parker Fitzgerald and Leo Patrone

NEW YORK

Published by Artisan
A division of Workman Publishing Company, Inc.
225 Varick Street
New York, NY 10014-4381
artisanbooks.com

Published simultaneously in Canada by Thomas Allen & Son, Limited

Library of Congress Cataloging-in-Publication Data

Williams, Nathan
  The kinfolk table : recipes for small gatherings / Nathan Williams.
     pages cm
  Includes index.
  ISBN 978-1-57965-532-7
  1. Dinners and dining. 2. Cooking. I. Title.
  TX737.W54 2013
  641.5'3—dc23   2013006294

Design by Amanda Jane Jones

Printed in China

10 9 8 7 6 5 4 3

CONTENTS

COPENHAGEN, DENMARK

THE ENGLISH COUNTRYSIDE

INTRODUCTION

NATHAN & KATIE WILLIAMS

{ FOUNDERS OF *KINFOLK* }

NATHAN: Since I was in high school, I've noticed a disconnect between both "home cooking" and "entertaining" and the ways my friends get together to share a meal. "Home cooking" sounds serious, even stodgy, and "entertaining" has a formal and frilly ring to it. Neither term describes what, in college, were quiet evenings spent making lasagne with a couple of close friends to jazz playing in the background. We gathered in a small apartment and cooked meals at least every other day, but we weren't pressing table linens, printing name cards, or brushing up on dining etiquette. We often used paper plates and stuck with the same fork for dessert that we had used for the main course, buttering baguettes with a paring knife so we would have fewer dishes to wash. Our formula for those evenings was to cook, eat, and talk. Nothing else was necessary.

So what can we call this tradition that has become such a valued part of our lives? It's not just "hanging out," which describes something careless and unintentional, and we're not having "dinner parties," a phrase that brings to mind events that are far too rigid, planned, and controlled to define the way we nourish ourselves. The idea for the magazine *Kinfolk* was born in the course of trying to describe those evenings spent with friends when the hours pass effortlessly, conversation flows naturally, cooking is participatory, and the evening ends with a satisfying sense of accomplishment. The fledgling *Kinfolk* had two goals: to offer an alternative idea of entertaining—casual, intentional, meaningful—and to make that kind of entertaining feel more natural and accessible to a younger crowd like my friends and me.

Our first objective has been to peel off the fluff and commercial layers that complicate entertaining. Next we have tried to put the social reasons for inviting friends into our homes— the relationships, traditions, community, and conversations—in the foreground and let the superficial details like fancy recipes and table decorations recede into the background. In retrospect, we didn't start the magazine as a strategic plan to fill a commercial void in the market. Frankly, *Kinfolk* was much more self-serving; we simply wanted a magazine that we

ourselves would be excited to pick up, a magazine that would resonate with us and our casual way of entertaining. Today *Kinfolk* is a consistent source of active, meaningful things to do for both our team and our readers, and the concept continues to grow with the quarterly print magazine, daily online stories, and in-person workshops, dinners, and events held around the world.

Each of those channels serves its own purpose. The quarterly print issues explore traditions and the reasons we gather together with in-depth essays and photo series. Our website is more focused on practical stories, with tips and tutorials teaching readers how to do things on their own. The event series provides settings for learning hands-on skills and meeting like-minded people in the different cities where readers live. These projects complement one another in offering ideas for things to cook, make, and do while promoting the deeper purpose of helping to build communities around ourselves.

This book applies the casual approach to entertaining depicted in our magazine to cooking and recipes. My hope is that it will find a place on cookbook shelves like my own, which are filled not just with classics and celebrity-chef volumes but also with the tattered, stained, spiral-bound little collections of family or neighborhood recipes put out by cooks I know and trust. Despite their humble appearance, these are the books that pack a punch with their recipes, and that's why they are my favorites. This book represents an effort to take the same

In each home we visited, the people living there reinforced my belief that "entertaining" has many more shapes and forms than what that term often brings to mind. It can be the most elaborate and boisterous thing in the world, and it can also be quiet, personal, and low-key, a meditative ritual we enjoy on our own. It can be planned, structured, and executed wonderfully, but it can also be last-minute, spontaneous, a team effort, and wonderfully imperfect.

communal neighborhood approach by welcoming you into the homes of our *Kinfolk* team, along with a diverse group of friends, family, contributing writers, artists, and other makers.

In the following pages you'll meet people with different vocations and avocations, from coffee connoisseur to food editor, interior designer to ceramicist, caterer to florist, as well as bakers, musicians, painters, photographers, food bloggers, fashion designers, restaurateurs, farmers, writers, coffee roasters, and even my sweet retired grandmother. They live on their own, as couples, and as families and represent the full adult life span in their ages. Each person was asked to contribute because he or she lives a life consistent with the simplicity we try to promote in our magazine, embodying a balanced, intentional way of living and a genuine appreciation of food and hosting friends in their homes. I visited their homes for this book in an effort to capture a glimpse of what I think makes them each remarkable, and in these homes I observed the passion with which they embrace the *Kinfolk* spirit. Morten Svendsen (page 148), for example, rebuilt the kitchen in his small Copenhagen flat so it could accommodate ten to fifteen of his friends for the meals he hosts there on a regular basis. Our friend Dusty Hume (page 216) often drives out from Portland to the Oregon coast on the weekends to collect fresh mussels before the sun rises, preparing them later for potluck dinners.

I can't help being excited to introduce you to all the people in this book because they seem to understand that good food and community are just as important as the careers in which they work, that the rituals and traditions that bring us together are essential to balanced lives. The people in these pages personify the fact that there's something to be said for slowing down, sitting back, and breathing deeply. In fact, I'm convinced that the creativity and success they all enjoy in their work is at least in part the result of a grounding focus on these humble things. To some, the hobbies they find most fulfilling have actually become sustainable careers. In Oregon, for example, Chris Siegel and Nolan Calisch (page 250) recently leased a property to begin an organic farm. And Sarah Winward (page 282), after years of dreaming up nature installations and flower arrangements, decided to set up shop and launch her own floral business in Salt Lake City.

From people like these three, who espouse a humble, down-to-earth way of entertaining that emphasizes nothing more than togetherness, you can expect to learn how a meal can be much more fulfilling when its preparation involves the friends who plan to sit down at the table. We all enjoy helping out, and the personal investment of contributing to a meal, even just tossing the salad, usually helps us enjoy the food even more. Then there are the rituals that

Entertaining looks different for all of us, but as long as we're cooking and inviting people into our homes with a genuine interest in sharing experiences, conversing, and eating together, then the way we do these things becomes insignificant and ultimately comes naturally. A burned dish or a missing serving piece becomes trivial. The humble soup or homely bread becomes a feast. It all seems quite simple.

cement a family, whether it's a couple or a clan of six. For Sam and Ashley Owens (page 54) that means playing loud music in the kitchen while preparing weekend breakfasts. For Ida Lærke (page 134), it entails passing on the tradition of smørrebrød, the beloved open-face Danish sandwiches, by making them with her young son, Saxo, almost every day.

A home with an open-door policy that friends find irresistible can be anywhere, yet place is integral to the traditions we grow. Ask anyone from Alberta, Canada, where I spent my childhood, about the harsh winters and windy summers and he or she will understand why it made sense for my group of friends to develop a habit of making food and enjoying dinners together as early as in high school. In the years since, I've found that each place I have visited has its own unique sense of communality, and that's what I hope to convey in the sections of this book, each of which represents a vibrant and nourishing place.

Brooklyn is represented by an eclectic mix of artisans and young food enthusiasts. Then there are my friends in Portland, Oregon, who often share their homes and talents for home cooking. People from the English countryside show us how to welcome friends and strangers with grace and charm—as well as with simple food prepared with the freshest ingredients. Denmark, with its long-held tradition of low-key hospitality, delighted me by having a word to describe experiences shared with loved ones in warmth, in candlelight, with good food: *hygge* (pronounced similarly to "hooga"), for which I wish we had a counterpart in English.

These far-flung parts of the world seem to value simplicity, hospitality, and balance, pursued with intentionality every day of the week. In this book I wanted to bring to life some of the individuals who live there and have something unique to share. So I packed my bags and departed along with two friends from our *Kinfolk* team to spend time with each person individually, observing them as they prepared their favorite recipes and talked about the traditions that matter most to them. We sat at their tables and asked questions to figure out how they tick and how we could emulate their warmth and hospitality. We scribbled notes with lessons, tips, and recipes to share here. I left each of their homes with a big, cheesy grin of satisfaction on my face and often stopped at the market for ingredients on my way home to replicate the dish I had just learned, like Lillie Auld's Pasta with Wilted Arugula, Almonds, and Soft Goat Cheese (page 52) and Mikkel Lippmann's simple cabbage salad, which he calls Spidskål (page 103). After every interview I was eager to get home, empowered to cook each dish myself and share it at my own table.

Like the traditions described by the contributors, the recipes carry special meaning for them, whether passed down from parents and earlier generations or go-to recipes that they make most often at home; these are their all-time favorites. They are dishes served at breakfast, lunch, and dinner, as snacks or with a cup of tea or coffee. There is a mix of simple to complex and light to hearty. The recipes even fit different group dynamics with servings for one, for two, and for a few. What impresses me most is how each recipe shared here carries memories and significance for the author and how that significance translated to enrich my own experience as I've made and enjoyed these dishes on my own.

Sharing meals, and everything that precedes those meals—whether it's growing some of the food or sourcing it locally, reading about and forming an intimate connection with the land, or lovingly preparing delicious ingredients—is central in the lives of these individuals. Their days pass with purpose, and they revere family and personal traditions with stalwart commitment while actively looking for new traditions to experience and include in their own repertoire. Their lives are enriched beyond measure as a result.

In each home we visited, the people living there reinforced my belief that "entertaining" has many more shapes and forms than what that term often brings to mind. It can be the most elaborate and boisterous thing in the world, and it can also be quiet, personal, and low-key, a meditative ritual we enjoy on our own. It can be planned, structured, and executed wonderfully, but it can also be last-minute, spontaneous, a team effort, and wonderfully imperfect.

Entertaining looks different for each of us, but as long as we're cooking and inviting people into our homes with a genuine interest in connecting, conversing, and eating together, then the way we do these things becomes insignificant and ultimately comes naturally. A burned dish or a missing serving piece becomes trivial. The humble soup or homely bread becomes a feast. It all seems quite simple. ◆

Shrimp Seviche
with Chili-Cumin Tortilla Chips

FOR THE SEVICHE

1 pound (455 grams) large shrimp, peeled and deveined

1 cucumber (about 8 ounces/ 230 grams), quartered and sliced

¼ medium red onion, thinly sliced

¼ cup (1 ounce/30 grams) fresh cilantro leaves, chopped

2 garlic cloves, minced

1 serrano chile, minced

½ cup (120 milliliters) fresh lime juice, from about 4 limes

2 tablespoons (30 milliliters) olive oil

Salt and freshly ground black pepper

FOR THE CHIPS

Three 8-inch (20-centimeter) flour tortillas

2 tablespoons (30 milliliters) fresh lime juice, from about 2 limes

1 teaspoon (0.1 ounce/3 grams) chili powder

½ teaspoon ground cumin

Coarse salt

FOR THE SEVICHE

Bring a large saucepan of water to a boil over medium-high heat. Cook the shrimp for about 3 minutes or until they turn opaque. Drain the shrimp and rinse them under cold running water to stop the cooking.

Combine the cucumber, onion, cilantro, garlic, chile, lime juice, and olive oil in a large bowl. Add the shrimp and toss to combine. Season with salt and pepper to taste. Cover the bowl with plastic wrap and refrigerate the seviche for about 2 hours to meld the flavors.

FOR THE CHIPS

Position a rack in the center of the oven and preheat the oven to 400°F (204°C).

Brush one side of each tortilla with the lime juice, then cut the tortillas into quarters or eighths, as desired. Arrange the tortillas in a single layer on a baking sheet.

Stir the chili powder, cumin, and ¼ teaspoon coarse salt in a small bowl and sprinkle over the tortillas.

Bake for about 10 minutes or until the chips are crisp and lightly browned. Transfer the sheet to a rack and cool completely. Season with salt to taste and serve with the chilled seviche.

Serves 6 to 8

Citrus Lentil Salad

1 cup (7 ounces/200 grams) dried lentils, picked over

6 scallions, white and pale green parts only, thinly sliced

3 tablespoons (45 milliliters) extra-virgin olive oil

1 tablespoon (15 milliliters) white wine or apple cider vinegar

3 tablespoons (45 milliliters) fresh lemon juice

Grated zest of 1 lemon or orange

1 tablespoon (0.45 ounce/ 13 grams) sugar

Salt and freshly ground black pepper

Rinse the lentils under cold running water in a fine-mesh sieve until the water runs clear. Place the lentils in a medium saucepan and add enough cold water to cover by 3 inches (7.6 centimeters). Bring to a boil, then reduce the heat to medium-low, cover, and simmer for 20 to 30 minutes or until the lentils are tender.

Drain the lentils and return them to the pot. Add enough cold water to cover by 3 inches (7.6 centimeters). Remove and discard any lentil shells that rise to the top, then drain once again.

Place the lentils in a large bowl and add the scallions, olive oil, vinegar, lemon juice, zest, sugar, and salt and pepper to taste.

Let the salad rest for at least 20 minutes to allow the flavors to combine. Serve. The salad can be stored, refrigerated, in an airtight container for up to 2 days.

Note: The scallions may be replaced by ½ red onion or 2 shallots, thinly sliced. The sugar may be replaced with agave syrup.

Serves 4

BROOKLYN

NEW YORK, USA

Brooklyn is an intricate mosaic. Residents come from myriad places, cultures, and traditions, yet even within this diverse mix they retain distinct personalities and modes of expression. I never have to be in Brooklyn for long to notice this exciting diversity, along with all the trends that I seem to have missed or that are still to come to my neck of the woods, three thousand miles to the west.

The first time I went to Brooklyn, I remember weaving through one stretch of shops where every door seemed to open into a world far from those streets. Hints of cumin and saffron here, garlic and chili powder there, with coffee wafting around each corner were the scents that greeted me. The combination of colors, sounds, and foods still makes it an experience unlike any other.

Just as Brooklyn's food scene includes a mix of world cuisines, I was not surprised to find that the friends I have met over the years and the dishes they have prepared for me reflect the variety of their home states and countries. This variety becomes vivid in the following pages, with the recipes they have chosen to share from their own families and traditions.

A hallmark of Brooklyn to me is the adventurous and fearless approach to creating meals that each of the people in this section takes. Many of the dishes we ate together as I visited their homes dotted around the borough were true to the heritage of the individual but had a novel flair or an unexpected pairing of flavors. I've come to admire this way of maintaining family favorites while encouraging food to evolve from generation to generation.

ARIEL DEARIE

{ FLORIST }

Ariel Dearie's world is literally spilling over with flowers, vines, and branches. From her shelves to kitchen counters, tables, and bookshelves, she uses arrangements of all shapes and types to bring natural beauty to every corner of her home. Her apartment, a cozy loft in Williamsburg, is home to her wild imagination and, naturally, her sprawling plant life. The sun throws slanted light through her tall windows, tracing her apartment with shadows of dangling vines and rounded vases.

"Each morning, no matter how busy, my mom allots an hour to reading the newspaper and drinking coffee at the kitchen counter. She has a whole system where she makes a cup of coffee, reads the front section, drinks half a cup, and then goes back and heats up the other half cup before returning to the paper. Whenever I go back to New Orleans I join her in this ritual, reading whatever newspaper section she allows me and savoring every moment." —ARIEL DEARIE

Ariel is a New Orleans native who migrated north for the inspiration and vibrancy of the Big City. A sweetly Southern soul, she now thrives up north as an accomplished florist, providing arrangements for weddings, special events, photo shoots, and even large dinner gatherings. In her own kitchen, her flowers find their place among little vases of herbs—white peonies among bunches of basil and sprigs of dill, for example. Flowers and herbs are perfectly at home together.

Ariel also connects the world of flowers with the world of food. To her, both flowers and food are at their best in their most natural state, springing from the local ground and maintaining their own organic, wild beauty. That beauty is translated to her treatment of the foods of her native Louisiana, the fish, garlic, onions, and butter that are at the center of many of her meals, which she lovingly prepares for her friends in Brooklyn. ◆

Barbecued Shrimp

24 jumbo shrimp, peeled with tails on

8 tablespoons (1 stick/ 113 grams) unsalted butter, cut into 8 pieces

¼ cup (60 milliliters) extra-virgin olive oil

1 tablespoon (0.5 ounce/ 45 milliliters) Cajun seasoning, such as Tony Chachere's

½ teaspoon salt

2 lemons, cut into 6 rounds, plus 1 tablespoon (15 milliliters) fresh lemon juice

2 fresh rosemary sprigs

6 garlic cloves, minced

ARIEL: *This is a classic New Orleans dish and was one of my favorites growing up. This particular dish is my dad's rendition of the original, which is said to have been created at Pascal's Manale restaurant.*
Serve this dish with hot, crusty bread.

Rinse the shrimp and pat them dry with paper towels. Arrange them in a single layer in a 13-by-9-inch (33-by-23-centimeter) baking dish. Scatter the butter pieces over the shrimp, then drizzle them with the olive oil. Sprinkle the Cajun seasoning, salt, and lemon juice over the shrimp.

Arrange the lemon slices and rosemary sprigs over the shrimp. Position a rack in the upper third of the oven and set the oven to broil. Broil the shrimp for 3 minutes, then remove the dish from the oven and stir to thoroughly combine the ingredients. Return the dish to the oven and repeat the procedure every 1 to 2 minutes until the shrimp are opaque and cooked through. Add the garlic to the dish, stir, and distribute the shrimp among 4 ramekins or bowls, spooning the sauce over them. Serve immediately.

Pictured on page 4
Serves 4

Open-Faced Sandwiches with Feta, Tomatoes, Capers, and Basil

1 baguette

2 tablespoons (30 milliliters) extra-virgin olive oil, plus additional for drizzling

2 tablespoons (30 milliliters) balsamic vinegar

8 ounces (230 grams) French sheep's-milk feta, cut into 8 slices

2 medium tomatoes, cut into 8 slices

1 medium red onion, thinly sliced

2 tablespoons (1 ounce/ 30 grams) drained capers

8 fresh basil leaves

Salt and freshly ground black pepper

ARIEL: *This dish is really great in the summer and for picnics. It's super simple and light, yet satisfying. When I was growing up, my family would pack these sandwiches and picnic by the Mississippi River.*

Cut the baguette in half crosswise, then cut each piece in half lengthwise. Drizzle the cut sides with the 2 tablespoons olive oil and the vinegar.

Arrange the feta slices in a single layer over the cut side of the 4 bread pieces, then top with the tomato slices, onion slices, capers, and basil. Drizzle with olive oil and season with salt and pepper to taste. Serve.

Pictured on page 5
Makes 4 open-faced sandwiches

MAX & ELI SUSSMAN

{ CHEFS }

Brooklyn, New York, is a long way from Detroit, Michigan, where the Sussman brothers grew up, but their journey to a shared passion for cooking has been a short one, beginning when they were teens with a "no rules" approach in a pro kitchen at summer camp. Today each holds a chef position at a respected Brooklyn restaurant: Max at Roberta's and Eli at Mile End delicatessen.

"When I was growing up, it was normal to have an entire side of our family come over for a brunch of bagels and lox and tuna fish and smoked fish and quiche. I love the idea that you wake up and everyone comes over to hang out."
—ELI SUSSMAN

Max and Eli communicate and navigate the kitchen with synchronicity. One lights the fire under a pot on the stove. A few minutes later the other turns and stirs what is simmering within. Soon after that the other approaches and lowers the heat. One is chatty and engaging, the other more reserved and intensely focused on his actions. Both effortlessly engage in conversation with the friends around them while cooking. When the work is finished, an impeccable dish emerges from the generous collaborative spirit among the brothers and their guests. ◆

Sweet Potato Hash with Italian Sausage and Poached Egg

FOR THE HASH

2 large sweet potatoes, peeled and cut into 1-inch pieces

Kosher salt and freshly ground black pepper

2 tablespoons (30 milliliters) olive or vegetable oil

½ medium yellow onion, thinly sliced

1 garlic clove, thinly sliced

1 dry pint (12 ounces/ 340 grams) heirloom tomatoes, coarsely chopped

2 ears corn, husked and shucked

1 bunch (6 ounces/170 grams) of baby red Russian kale, chopped

2 tablespoons (1 ounce/ 30 grams) unsalted butter

⅓ cup (0.4 ounce/12 grams) fresh herbs, such as thyme, chives, chervil, or flat-leaf parsley, finely chopped

ELI & MAX: *This dish is a complete meal. But if you are looking for something a little lighter, the hash and poached egg can stand on their own without the sausage, and that way it's vegetarian, too.*

FOR THE HASH

Place the sweet potatoes and 2 teaspoons (12 grams) salt in a large saucepan and add enough cold water to cover by 1 inch (2.5 centimeters). Bring to a boil over medium-high heat, then reduce the heat to medium. Simmer for about 10 minutes or until the sweet potatoes are tender; drain.

Heat the oil in a large seasoned cast-iron skillet over medium heat until it begins to shimmer. Add the sweet potatoes and onion and allow them to cook without stirring for 3 to 4 minutes or until they begin to brown. Continue to cook them, stirring occasionally, for 3 to 4 minutes longer. Stir in the garlic and cook for 1 minute or until fragrant. Stir in the tomatoes and corn and cook, stirring, for about 3 minutes or until the kernels are tender and the tomatoes have softened. Stir in the kale and cook for 2 minutes or until wilted. Stir in the butter and season with salt and pepper to taste. Stir in the fresh herbs.

FOR THE SAUSAGE, EGGS, AND TOAST

1 teaspoon (5 milliliters) olive or vegetable oil

2 links (8 ounces/230 grams) sweet Italian sausage

2 cups (480 milliliters) water

¼ cup (60 milliliters) white vinegar

2 teaspoons (12 grams) kosher salt

2 large eggs

4 slices crusty sourdough bread

Unsalted butter

FOR THE SAUSAGE, EGGS, AND TOAST

While the hash is cooking, heat the oil in a medium skillet over medium heat until it begins to shimmer. Poke the sausages all over with a fork, then cook, turning occasionally, for about 8 minutes or until browned and cooked through.

Bring the water, vinegar, and salt to a boil in a small saucepan over medium-high heat. Reduce the heat to low and allow the water to come to a simmer.

Crack the eggs into two ramekins. Swirl the water and immediately, carefully, drop the eggs in, one at a time. Cook them for 2 to 3 minutes or until the whites become opaque. Transfer them to a paper-towel-lined plate with a slotted spoon.

Toast the bread slices and butter to taste.

To serve, place half of the hash on each of two plates, then top with an egg. Serve with the sausage and toast.

Serves 2

Plum and Cilantro Salad with Fresh Goat Cheese

4 ripe plums, cut into wedges

1 cup (1 ounce/30 grams) baby spinach leaves, washed

⅓ cup (3½ ounces/100 grams) French breakfast radishes, thinly sliced

2 tablespoons (30 milliliters) white balsamic vinegar

2 tablespoons (30 milliliters) extra-virgin olive oil

Salt

4 ounces (115 grams) fresh goat cheese

¼ cup (0.4 ounce/10 grams) fresh cilantro leaves

ELI & MAX: *With its beautiful colors and fresh flavors, this salad is an ode to the beginning of summer. Try to get everything at your farmers' market, even if that means making substitutions. That is part of the fun and excitement of cooking seasonally!*

If the radish greens are tender enough, slice them and add them to the salad as well.

Toss the plums, spinach, and radishes together in a large bowl.

Whisk the vinegar and olive oil in a small bowl until well combined and season with salt to taste. Drizzle enough vinaigrette over the salad to dress it lightly. Divide the salad evenly among four plates and top it with the goat cheese and cilantro. Serve immediately with the remaining vinaigrette if desired.

Serves 4 as an appetizer

WILLIAM HEREFORD &
ALYSSA PAGANO

{ PHOTOGRAPHER AND STYLIST }

William Hereford's photography combines the best of traditional film and the best of modern technology. His product, both stills and motion, is classical and familiar. His technique, however, is cutting-edge. He is not constrained by traditional camera definitions but instead works within a continuum between photography and cinematography. His work is fluid no matter the format, from tablet to computer to television.

In person, William is refreshingly down-to-earth. He was raised in Virginia, and his commonwealth roots manifest themselves in a classical American ruggedness, an easy closeness to the land and its fruits. While he may now live in Brooklyn, he has not compromised his pastoral aesthetic or tastes. His food photography begins with capturing dishes, and ends with shots of chickens, butcheries, and whitewashed farmhouses—but he doesn't stop there. His work captures a spirit in his subjects, be it the lowliest of old farms or the grandest of New York fine-dining establishments. William gives each one life and meaning.

When it comes to food, what gives meaning to William's meals is his ability to connect with the food's source and the work that has been poured into it. It is one thing to enjoy a taste, but it is another thing altogether to understand the taste and the work behind it. William and his girlfriend, Alyssa Pagano, try to source their ingredients locally and with the season. But when that isn't possible, they find comfort and warmth in using what's available to make a pot of soup, sharing in its bounty together. They cherish their time over meals, for the simple enjoyment of the food and for the conversation that unspools over it.

"Burnt tomatoes have been included in every Thanksgiving and Christmas dinner since before I was born. Ironically, I hated them for a good bit of my childhood, simply because the dish looked sophisticated and grown-up. Though a Virginia native, I went to college in Maine and currently live in Brooklyn, so my Southern drawl has dwindled over the years. My mother's has not. I will always remember her politely demanding 'more bernt tamatas, please.'"

—WILLIAM HEREFORD

Burnt Tomatoes

3 tablespoons (42 grams) unsalted butter, softened

6 pounds (2.7 kilograms) vine-ripe tomatoes

Salt and freshly ground black pepper

3 cups (15 ounces/420 grams) all-purpose flour

⅓ cup (80 milliliters) vegetable oil, plus additional as needed

1 tablespoon (0.45 ounce/ 13 grams) sugar

Position a rack in the center of the oven and preheat the oven to 325°F (163°C). Grease a 13-by-9-inch (33-by-23-centimeter) baking dish with the butter.

Slice the tomatoes ½ inch (1.28 centimeters) thick and season with salt and pepper. Spread the flour on a large plate and dredge the tomato slices, shaking off the excess.

Heat the oil in a large skillet over medium heat until shimmering. Fry the tomato slices in batches, adding as many to the skillet as will fit in a single layer, about 3 minutes per side, or until they turn crisp and golden. Using a slotted spatula, transfer the tomatoes to the prepared baking dish, arranging them in a single layer. Sprinkle the tomatoes with 1 teaspoon (4 grams) of the sugar.

Repeat the frying procedure with additional tomatoes, adding more oil as needed. If the flour sediment begins to burn, discard the oil, wipe out the pan, and heat fresh oil before continuing.

Sprinkle the second layer of tomatoes with another teaspoon (4 grams) of the sugar, repeat the tomato frying and layering procedure, and finish with the remaining 1 teaspoon (4 grams) sugar.

Bake the tomatoes for 1 hour or until soft and bubbling. Transfer the dish to a rack and cool for 10 minutes. Serve.

Serves 10 to 12

DAVID QUON,
DEREK VAN HEULE &
NATHAN WARKENTIN

{ MUSICIANS }

The band We Barbarians is composed of David Quon, Derek Van Heule, and Nathan Warkentin, and together they form a rare and inspiring musical dynamic. The guys met one another in Los Angeles and have now been playing together for over a decade. They have produced numerous records and survived a cross-country move to Greenpoint, Brooklyn, in the process. While their music has been described as indie and bluesy rock, the little community they've created together is quite possibly without classification. David, Derek, and Nathan not only spend their working hours together, but also live together, cook together, and host together, much the way a family does. Their common California past comes through in their cooking, most notably in the avocado slices placed on anything they prepare. The spirit of their Brooklyn present comes through in how they source their food, demonstrated by the rooftop gardens where they grow their vegetables and the corner bakery where they pick up fresh brioche buns. Regardless of location, however, these guys love a cookout and know how to do one well. A casual backyard barbecue is one of the simplest forms of entertaining, and David, Derek, and Nathan agree that it is perhaps one of the most social.

Accordingly, they fired up the grill for us, serving char-grilled turkey burgers, chips and guacamole, and glasses of cold sangria on the side. Our dining experience with these musicians felt like a truly American one—spent outside under the hot summer sun, among effusive and hilarious company. It felt not unlike those fondly remembered family cookouts from growing up, enjoyed in the comfort of the familiar and the ease of just being with one another. ◆

Mexican-Style BBQ Corn

4 large ears of corn

1 tablespoon (½ ounce/
14 grams) unsalted butter,
melted

¼ cup (60 grams) mayonnaise

2 teaspoons (0.3 ounce/9 grams)
sriracha

2 ounces (60 grams) cotija
cheese, crumbled

Light a charcoal grill and allow the coals to turn ashy and white.
If using a gas grill, heat it to medium-high.

Peel the husks back from the corn, leaving them attached to the base
of the corncobs, then remove the silk. Brush the corn with the melted
butter, then cover with the husks. Cook the corn on the grill for 15 to
20 minutes or until tender, turning frequently. Transfer the corn to a
platter.

Stir the mayonnaise and sriracha together. Peel back the husks,
spread the spicy mayonnaise all over the corn, then sprinkle with the
cheese. Serve immediately.

Serves 4

Quinoa and Bean Summer Salad

1 cup (7 ounces/200 grams)
quinoa

2 tablespoons (30 milliliters)
extra-virgin olive oil

Sea salt

2 cups (480 milliliters) water

One 16-ounce (455-gram) can
black beans, rinsed and drained

One 16-ounce (455-gram) can
chickpeas, rinsed and drained

1 red bell pepper, ribs and seeds
removed, chopped

1 cucumber, seeded and cut into
¼-inch (0.64-centimeter) dice

¼ cup (60 milliliters) red wine
vinegar

2 tablespoons (30 milliliters)
fresh lemon juice

Freshly ground black pepper

Rinse the quinoa under cold running water in a fine-mesh sieve until
the water runs clear. Heat 1 tablespoon (15 milliliters) of the olive
oil in a medium saucepan over medium-high heat until shimmering.
Add the quinoa and ½ teaspoon salt and cook, stirring, for about
5 minutes or until beginning to dry and turn golden. Add the water
and bring to a boil. Reduce the heat to medium and simmer for
about 10 minutes or until most of the water has evaporated. Reduce
the heat to low, cover, and cook for about 15 minutes, until all of the
water has been absorbed and the quinoa is tender. Fluff the quinoa
with a fork and transfer to a salad bowl. Cool completely.

Add the black beans, chickpeas, bell pepper, cucumber, vinegar,
lemon juice, and remaining 1 tablespoon (15 milliliters) olive oil and
toss to combine. Season with salt and pepper to taste and serve.

Serves 4

Turkey Avocado Burgers

1¼ pounds (500 grams) lean ground turkey

2 to 3 garlic scapes, minced (about ¼ cup/57 grams)

1 tablespoon (15 milliliters) extra-virgin olive oil

1 teaspoon (3 grams) ground cumin

1 teaspoon (6 grams) salt

1 teaspoon (6 grams) freshly ground black pepper

4 brioche rolls, halved

Gruyère cheese slices

2 ripe avocados, pitted and sliced

Mustard greens

Light a charcoal grill and allow the coals to turn ashy and white. If using a gas grill, heat it to medium-high.

Combine the turkey, garlic scapes, olive oil, cumin, salt, and pepper in a medium bowl and mix until well combined. Shape the mixture into 4 patties and grill for 4 to 5 minutes per side or until cooked through.

Serve the burgers on the brioche rolls and top with Gruyère cheese slices, avocado slices, and mustard greens.

Serves 4

Citrus-Mint Sangria

One 750-milliliter bottle Gewürztraminer, chilled

¼ cup (60 milliliters) Cointreau

1 grapefruit, scrubbed, halved, seeded, and cut into slices ¼ inch (0.64 centimeter) thick

1 orange, scrubbed, seeded, and cut into slices ¼ inch (0.64 centimeter) thick

1 lemon, scrubbed, seeded, and cut into slices ¼ inch (0.64 centimeter) thick

Ice cubes

Fresh mint leaves

Combine the wine, Cointreau, grapefruit, orange, and lemon in a pitcher and stir. Refrigerate for at least 1 hour or until thoroughly chilled.

Serve over ice with mint leaves.

Makes 1 pitcher (about 32 ounces/950 milliliters)

ELIZABETH HADDAD

{ COFFEE CONNOISSEUR/BLOGGER }

Perhaps before she even realized it, coffee found Elizabeth Haddad. As a child, she sat alongside her mother and her mother's friends as they sipped coffee together. She recalls wanting to be a part of those experiences, even if she didn't yet have a palate for the bitter beans. She remembers the porcelain cups and the lipstick stains around the rims, and the particular joy of sharing a cup of coffee has followed Elizabeth into adulthood.

One day, while sipping an exquisitely perfect cappuccino at a streetside café in Rome, Elizabeth found this enduring fascination with coffee coming full circle. She understood at that moment

"I was always the resident coffee maker in my household. School mornings, Christmas morning, Easter morning, birthdays, holidays, weekends— all of my favorite memories take place in the morning over coffee with my friends and family. Obviously, my coffee ritual has grown in technicalities, with grinders and pour-overs and AeroPresses, yet the essence is still the same."
—ELIZABETH HADDAD

that in cultures around the world, life takes place over mugs and French presses. And so began her blog, *The Coffee Experiment*, a study and documentation of the varieties of coffee and the way coffee stimulates social interaction. As she has discovered and recorded, the enjoyment of this substance can also foster joy, community, and cultural expression.

Her personal coffee rituals are sacred and savored. They instill peace before a busy day and permit reflection in a distracting world. Brewing and sharing coffee is Elizabeth's way of centering herself, but also of connecting with others. While she currently resides in New York, Elizabeth travels far and wide to meet other coffee connoisseurs and long-distance friends over the best cup of joe in whatever town she may be visiting. ◆

Nanny Frannie's Apple Strudel

FOR THE PHYLLO DOUGH

4 cups (20 ounces/560 grams)
all-purpose flour, plus additional
for dusting

1 teaspoon (0.2 ounce/6 grams)
salt

1½ to 1¾ cups (355 to
415 milliliters) warm water

¼ cup (60 milliliters) extra-
virgin olive oil, plus additional
to coat the dough ball

1 tablespoon (15 milliliters)
fresh lemon juice

ELIZABETH: *My maternal grandmother, Frances, was my best friend growing up. We called her Nanny, because it rhymed with her nickname, Frannie. She was an avid Scrabble player, and I believe that our long hours of playing Scrabble together—our shared love of words—helped shape my future as a writer. She also taught me to sew and how to make a spoon stick to my nose. She was an amazing cook, constantly attempting to feed you at all hours of the day. We both had a love of fruit, and when I was a child she would cut fresh fruit for me all day long—kiwis, apples, strawberries, grapefruit. Though it seems simple, she could cut and peel fruit with such expertise that it was simply perfect. No one could peel an apple as fast, as neatly, and as thinly as Nanny could. Definitely a skill.*

Nanny would bring this apple strudel every time she came to our house. Now that I've made it a few times, I still don't know how she got the dough rolled out so large and thin. She would sometimes include raisins, but for some reason I despised raisins as a child, so she'd often make an "all fruit" one for me. Now that I'm older (and love raisins!), I've experimented with many different combinations; in the summer one can add blueberries or rhubarb, and in the fall or winter I've even added pumpkin. My fiancé (who will be my husband by the time this is published) is highly allergic to all nuts, so I make this nut-free. But I have to admit, this tastes amazing with walnuts or pecans.

FOR THE PHYLLO DOUGH

Combine the flour and salt in the bowl of a stand mixer fitted with the dough hook. Combine 1½ cups (355 milliliters) of the water, the olive oil, and the lemon juice in a liquid measuring cup. Using your fingertips, create a well in the center of the flour mixture and pour in the water mixture. With the mixer on medium-low speed, mix the ingredients until a soft dough is formed, adding more warm water if it appears too dry.

Knead on medium speed for about 10 minutes or until smooth. If kneading by hand, turn the dough out onto a clean, dry work surface dusted with flour. Shape the dough into a ball, brush with olive oil, place in a large bowl, and allow to rest, covered and at room temperature, for 1½ hours.

Cut the dough into 10 approximately 3-inch (7.6-centimeter) sections and cover them with a damp (but not wet) dish towel. One section of dough at a time, begin rolling the dough out with a floured rolling pin to about 15 by 13 inches (38 by 33 centimeters). As the dough begins to extend and thin out, sprinkle it with flour,

FOR THE FILLING

5 medium Gala or Granny Smith apples, peeled, cored, and cut into slices ⅛ inch (3 centimeters) thick

1 cup (5½ ounces/156 grams) fresh blueberries

2 tablespoons (14 grams) honey, or to taste

1 tablespoon (15 milliliters) fresh lemon juice

5½ tablespoons (2¾ ounces/ 80 grams) sugar, plus additional for sprinkling

1 teaspoon (0.1 ounce/3 grams) ground cinnamon, or to taste

8 tablespoons (1 stick/ 113 grams) unsalted butter, melted and cooled slightly

lifting it slightly with the rolling pin to dust the work surface as well. Roll the dough over the rolling pin, as if you were wrapping it in the dough, and once it's completely wrapped, unroll it and begin the process again, adding more flour as needed. The dough should be thin and translucent.

Set the completed dough aside and cover with a second damp dish towel. Repeat the rolling procedure with the remaining sections of dough and flour, laying the pieces of completed phyllo on top of each other, keeping them covered with the damp towel.

FOR THE FILLING AND ASSEMBLY

Position a rack in the center of the oven and preheat the oven to 400°F (204°C).

Combine the apples, blueberries, honey, lemon juice, sugar, and cinnamon in large bowl, tossing to combine. Allow the mixture to rest for 15 minutes or until the apples release their juices.

Lay a large sheet of parchment paper on a baking sheet. Arrange one sheet of phyllo on the paper, then brush it with butter and sprinkle with 1½ teaspoons (9 grams) sugar. Repeat the procedure with 4 more sheets of phyllo, the remaining butter, and the remaining 3 tablespoons (45 grams) sugar. (Roll out the remaining 5 pieces of phyllo, wrap them in parchment paper, then in plastic wrap, and freeze until needed; see Note.)

Arrange the apple filling in a 2-inch (5-centimeter) line down the center of the phyllo, leaving a 1-inch (2.5-centimeter) border at the top and bottom. Use the parchment paper to help fold the dough over just beyond the filling. Continue using the parchment paper to roll the phyllo into a compact rectangular package. Fold and tuck the ends under the strudel, then brush the top with butter and sprinkle with sugar.

Bake the strudel for 15 to 20 minutes or until it is golden brown. Transfer the sheet to a rack and cool for 15 minutes. Cut into pieces and serve.

Note: To use frozen phyllo, thaw the rolls in the refrigerator for 4 to 6 hours, then unroll, cover with a damp dish towel, and proceed with the recipe.

Pictured on page 31
Serves 6 to 8

AMY MERRICK

{ FLORIST/STYLIST }

As a child, Amy Merrick manned a farm stand alongside her sister, selling her father's tomato crop. Raised with flora and fauna on all sides in an endearing farmhouse nestled in the tiny town of Hancock, New Hampshire, she grew up more comfortable outside than in. Today she lives in an utterly different environment—Brooklyn, New York. Despite the radical change in surroundings, she remains the same, the steadfast product of her family and her childhood home.

Amy is an accomplished florist, writer, and stylist who uses the naturally untamed forms of twigs, blooms, and leaves to create arrangements that evoke more passion than propriety. Her aesthetic

"Spending a lot of time in a rural setting as a girl cemented my appreciation for the natural world, and moving to a big city really made me actively seek out ways to reconnect with that. Flowers made sense from the beginning."
—AMY MERRICK

is clearly drawn from her life in the country, but it's perfectly at home in the city, whether it is illuminating a special event, a photo shoot, or a wedding.

Although Amy has found a haven in her home and studio in Brooklyn, she retreats as often as she can to the pastoral lands of her childhood. This is where we met her, picked blueberries with her, and toured her family's farmhouse, the creak of weary wood floors under our feet. She filled our time together with stories of life there as she ladled jam into jars on the antique range. Her experience of New Hampshire is certainly not of this era. It is slow and tempered, focused almost exclusively on family and history. Amy is effortless here, and it seems to be this place that imbues her with the ability to translate the beauty, slowness, and extravagance of nature to her floral designs with similar ease. ◆

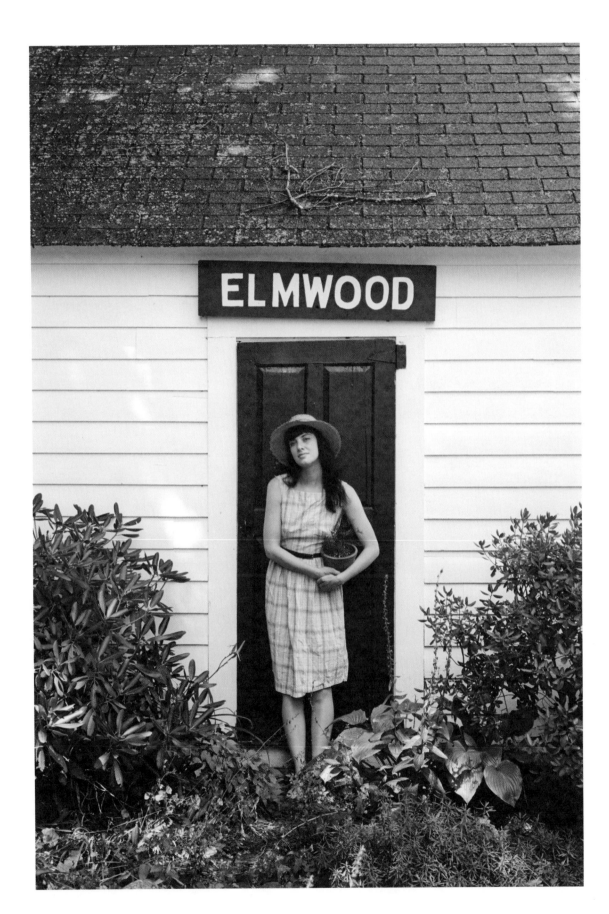

Wild Blueberry Currant Jam

1 cup (7 ounces/200 grams)
sugar

2 teaspoons (⅛ ounce/3 grams)
low-sugar pectin powder (see
Note)

6 cups (30 ounces/850 grams)
fresh blueberries, mashed

2 cups (14 ounces/400 grams)
red currants, mashed

¼ cup (60 milliliters) fresh
lemon juice

2 teaspoons (10 milliliters)
calcium water (see Note)

AMY: *Every year at the end of July when the wild blueberries ripen along the pond in New Hampshire, my family collects them to make jam. Sometimes I'll add currants if the season allows, because they have a nice tang and a lot of natural pectin to help the jam set. On wheat toast with ricotta or mixed into yogurt in the morning, it's a nice way to remember summer throughout the year.*

Sterilize three 16-ounce (480-milliliter) canning jars and lids in a hot water bath.

Combine the sugar and pectin in a mixing bowl.

Put the fruit and lemon juice in a saucepan and add the calcium water. Bring the fruit to a boil, then gradually pour in the sugar mixture, stirring constantly until dissolved, about 2 minutes. Bring the fruit back to a boil and remove from the heat.

Fill the canning jars, clean the jar rims thoroughly, and put on the lids, not screwing them on too tightly.

Submerge the jars in a large pot of boiling water and boil for 10 minutes. Remove and let the jars cool. Check that the lids are a little concave (a vacuum has been created) and refrigerate any that haven't sealed properly for immediate use.

Note: Amy likes Pomona's pectin, which uses calcium to set the jam rather than requiring it to contain a lot more sugar. A calcium powder packet comes in the box; follow the directions to make the calcium water (½ teaspoon calcium powder mixed with ½ cup water until dissolved) and store what you're not using here in the refrigerator—it will last a couple of months.

Pictured on pages 37 and 41
Makes 48 ounces/1.4 kilograms

NICK FAUCHALD

{ FOOD WRITER/PUBLISHER }

Nick Fauchald is a food world insider. He has led editorial teams for publications like *Food & Wine* and *Wine Spectator* and for other culinary-related projects. Most recently, he spent three years as editor in chief at *The Tasting Table*, a daily e-mail journal that offers subscribers a discerning look at the best recipes, chefs, and restaurants in their area. After years of working in print and then digital journalism, he is today combining these methods of communication in new and innovative ways. He is currently hard at work on developing products for both print and Web platforms, along with e-books, apps, and the old bread-and-butter cookbooks. Nick has consistently adapted to

---

"For me to truly enjoy myself in the kitchen, cooking must be a spontaneous activity. I don't like to think too much about what I'm going to cook ahead of time— even when I'm at the market—because then the logistical part of my brain takes over and the very small creative part gets kicked aside. But if I start cooking a dish not knowing where it will end up, I'll have no choice but to improvise. I do this partly because of the rush it gives me, but also because it keeps me true to the ingredients with which I'm cooking." —NICK FAUCHALD

---

the changing climate of readership and the demands of globalized platforms. He approaches journalism strategically, meeting the needs of the consumer through the increasingly diverse ways of reaching them.

Stemming from his wealth of experience, Nick is a professional in matters relating to the culinary world. He knows how to masterfully write a recipe yet can also break it down to let the simplest ingredients speak for themselves. His greatest quality, however, may be his focus on the importance of food when it comes to family gatherings or hosting in his own home, a philosophy born of a tradition of family meals together.

The food Nick made for us (including a peanut butter and bacon sandwich, shared here) was comforting and simple, neither complex nor intimidating. Our afternoon visit with him confirmed that Nick has the uncanny ability to keep audiences—whether those around his own dinner table or the far-flung beneficiaries of his writing endeavors—hungry for more. ◆

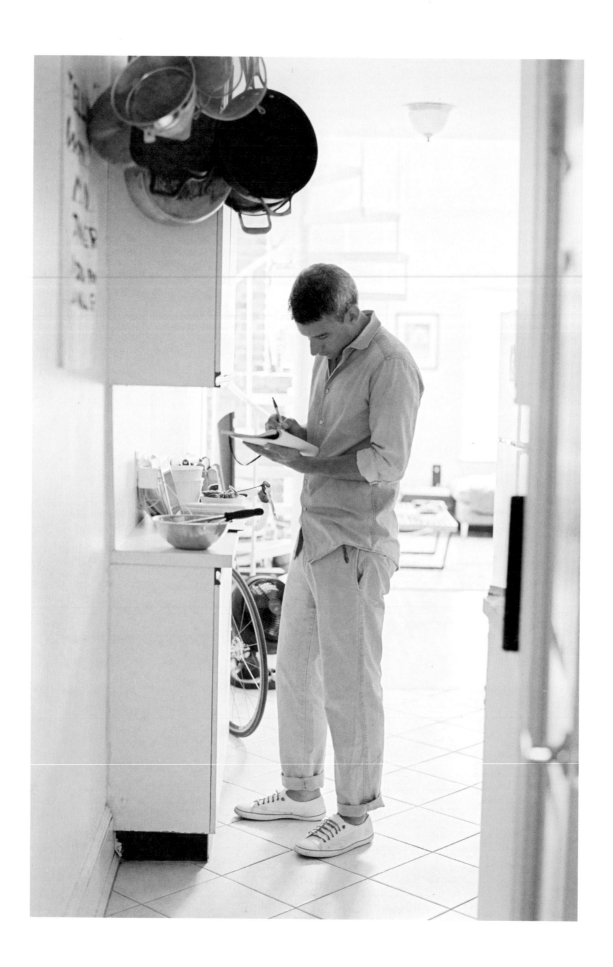

Pimento Cheese

1 pound (455 grams) sharp Cheddar cheese, coarsely grated

1 cup (5 ounces/140 grams) drained Peppadew peppers, finely chopped

½ cup (4 ounces/115 grams) chopped garlic dill pickles, plus pickle juice to taste

⅓ cup (2.6 ounces/75 grams) mayonnaise, plus additional as needed

½ small shallot, finely grated

2 tablespoons (30 grams) crème fraîche or sour cream

1 scallion, finely chopped

Salt and freshly ground black pepper

Tabasco sauce

Crackers or crostini, for serving

NICK: *I don't like to cook the same thing twice. Ever. But pimento cheese appears frequently at my dinners. It is the meat loaf of appetizers: a good vessel for combining leftover scraps found in your refrigerator. I've added all styles of pickles to the mix, experimented with roasted peppers and Peppadews (my favorite) in place of jarred pimentos, and tried it with myriad cheeses. And I always set some aside for pimento grilled cheese sandwiches.*

Combine the cheese, peppers, pickles, mayonnaise, shallot, crème fraîche, and scallion in a medium bowl and mix with a fork until well combined. Add more mayonnaise, 1 tablespoon (15 grams) at a time, to adjust the consistency to taste. The mixture should be thick but spreadable. Season with salt, pepper, Tabasco, and pickle juice to taste. Refrigerate in an airtight container until ready to use, for up to 1 week. Bring to room temperature prior to serving with crackers or crostini.

Pictured on page 45
Makes about 2 cups

Peanut Butter and Bacon Sandwiches

8 slices (about 8 ounces/ 230 grams) thick-cut bacon

8 slices Pullman loaf

Peanut butter

Honey (optional)

NICK: *When I was growing up, my father worked at the hospital located a block from our house, and most days he would come home for lunch. My mother would make these sandwiches for us at least once a week. I don't know when or why she started making PB&B sandwiches, nor from where her recipe came. (I think it's best, sometimes, not to know these things.)*

The trick is to make the bacon very crisp (my mother did it by using a microwave and lots of paper towels; I do it by starting the cooking in a cold cast-iron skillet) and to spread the peanut butter on the toast while the bread is still warm, so that the peanut butter melts just slightly before you eat it.

Cook the bacon in a cast-iron or large skillet over medium-low heat for about 8 minutes or until the bacon is very crisp. Drain it on paper towels, leaving 1 tablespoon (15 milliliters) of the bacon fat in the pan; reserve the rest. Cut the bacon slices in half crosswise.

Working in batches, toast the bread in the bacon fat over medium heat for about 2 minutes per side or until golden, adding the reserved fat as needed.

Spread peanut butter to taste on one piece of toast. Top with four pieces of bacon and drizzle with honey if desired. Top with a second piece of toast and cut the sandwich in half. Repeat with the remaining bread and bacon, additional peanut butter, and honey. Serve immediately.

Pictured on page 43
Makes 4 sandwiches

LILLIE AULD

{ BLOGGER/EVENT PLANNER }

Everyone loves a pie, and no one espouses this love more than Lillie Auld. She lives for pie, along with the entire spectrum of baked goods. Lillie runs the blog *Butter Me Up, Brooklyn!*, aptly named for the sugary, buttery treats that come out of her oven and end up in her blog as mouthwatering photographs and recipes. Her Internet space is brimming with recipes for all types of sweet treats—pies, tarts, cookies, brownies, mini doughnut muffins, and the occasional, as she calls it, "boozy drink." But she doesn't stop there. She shares small stories about growing up, as well as reflections on her current life in New York—anecdotes that are dry-witted and humble. Lillie's recipes are simple and delightful, and her voice is infectious. Her

---

"I try never to bake the same thing twice. Of course, this is difficult to achieve all the time, and my mom's tart at Christmas Eve is the exception to this rule, but I think it is important to continually try new ideas and explore unique flavors in baked goods." —LILLIE AULD

---

culinary expertise paired with her undeniable ability to make human connections earned her site the title of Best Baking and Desserts Blog from Saveur.com in 2012.

When Lillie is not baking or writing or photographing for her blog, she works as a freelance event planner for a variety of occasions, both large and small. She grew up in a large family, where even the simplest of gatherings was a spectacular affair. Her family's doors were always open, and it seemed there was always someone waiting at the threshold. Lillie learned at a young age that good food and good sweets ensure that people come a-calling. Of course, they come because the tastes are pleasing, but even more so because the experience of being together and sharing in something is powerful.

Lillie currently creates her recipes and baked goodies in her tiny city kitchen, which translates to a lack of counter space, cabinet storage, and helpful appliances. But these minor obstacles do not daunt her spirit. She keeps baking, and friends keep coming, which is a joy to those invited and a constant joy to Lillie herself. ◆

Pasta with Wilted Arugula, Almonds, and Soft Goat Cheese

Salt

½ cup (2 ounces/60 grams) sliced almonds

⅓ cup (80 milliliters) olive oil

3 garlic cloves, very thinly sliced

8 ounces (230 grams) short pasta such as fusilli, penne, or tortiglioni

4 cups (4 ounces/115 grams) arugula

4 ounces (115 grams) goat cheese

Freshly ground black pepper

Bring a large pot of water and 1 tablespoon (0.63 ounce/18 grams) salt to a boil over medium-high heat.

Meanwhile, toast the almonds in a large skillet over medium-high heat for about 5 minutes, stirring occasionally, until golden brown. Transfer the almonds to a small bowl.

Heat the olive oil in the same skillet over medium-high heat until shimmering. Add the garlic and cook, stirring and turning over, for 2 to 3 minutes or until lightly browned. With a slotted spoon, transfer the garlic chips to a paper-towel-lined plate and reserve the oil.

Boil the pasta for about 12 minutes or until al dente. While the pasta cooks, cook the arugula in the garlic oil over medium heat, stirring, for about 3 minutes or until wilted. Remove the skillet from the heat.

Reserve 1 cup (240 milliliters) of the pasta cooking water, then drain the pasta and return it to the pot. With a slotted spoon, transfer the arugula to the pasta, adding the cooking oil to taste. Add half of the goat cheese and 2 tablespoons (30 milliliters) of the reserved pasta water and stir until the cheese melts and achieves a saucelike consistency. Stir in additional pasta water to adjust the consistency to taste.

Stir the remaining half of the goat cheese and 1 tablespoon (15 milliliters) of the reserved pasta water together in a small bowl. Season the pasta with salt and pepper, then transfer to two serving bowls. Sprinkle the pasta with the almonds and garlic chips and dollop with the soft goat cheese. Serve immediately.

Serves 2

Almond-Jam Tart
(Linzer Torte)

Adapted from Lillie's mother, Mary Etue Auld, who adapted it from a 1977 issue of *Sunset* magazine

9 tablespoons (4½ ounces/ 126 grams) unsalted butter, at room temperature

1¾ cups (8¾ ounces/250 grams) all-purpose flour

1¾ cups (7 ounces/200 grams) almond flour

½ teaspoon baking powder

½ teaspoon salt

⅔ cup (4.6 ounces/130 grams) sugar

1 large egg, at room temperature

½ teaspoon vanilla extract

¼ teaspoon almond extract

12 ounces (340 grams) high-quality raspberry jam

Sliced almonds

Coarse sugar

Confectioners' sugar

Position a rack in the center of the oven and preheat the oven to 350°F (177°C). Grease a 9-inch (23-centimeter) tart pan with a removable bottom with 1 tablespoon (14 grams) of the butter.

Combine the flour, almond flour, baking powder, and salt in a medium bowl.

Beat the remaining 8 tablespoons (114 grams) butter and the sugar with an electric mixer on medium speed until light and fluffy, about 3 minutes. Scrape down the sides of the bowl with a rubber spatula, then add the egg and beat until fully incorporated. Add the vanilla and almond extracts and beat just until incorporated.

Press two-thirds of the dough into the bottom and up the sides of the tart pan. Spread the jam evenly over the dough.

Roll the remaining dough into a cylinder about 9 inches (23 centimeters) long and slice it into rounds ¼ inch (0.64 centimeter) thick. Arrange the rounds on top of the jam, slightly overlapping them, starting from the edge of the tart and working toward the center. Sprinkle the tart with the sliced almonds and coarse sugar.

Bake for 35 to 40 minutes or until the jam filling is bubbling and the dough rounds are lightly browned. Transfer the tart to a rack and cool completely, about 1 hour. Remove the tart from the pan, transfer it to a serving plate, and sift confectioners' sugar over it. Serve.

Pictured on pages 50 and 51
Serves 10

SAM & ASHLEY OWENS

{ MUSICIAN/ARTIST AND FASHION DESIGNER }

The subdued mien of both Sam and Ashley Owens is deceptive, their laid-back disposition occasionally disrupted by a burst of excitement. Both adept storytellers, they frequently recount memories of the culinary and family traditions that were part of their childhoods— mass pie bakings, special-edition family cookbooks, and family parades; the experiences are varied and treasured. It is fitting, then, that both are immersed in professions that necessitate a keen storytelling ability—Sam as a musician and mixed-media artist and Ashley as a fashion designer.

"We are shaped by all the things we come in contact with, and we always want to make sense of them. We are given a choice of what we do with all those raw materials and stimuli. I suppose I've always tried to make sense of it through making art and music, where others might make sense of it by plowing a field or building a building. . . . Maybe I should plow a field." —SAM OWENS

Legacy is woven into their creative work. Ashley's classically designed women's suits are inspired by her having grown up during the eighties, the era of the Power Suit. She relies on quality cashmeres and strong lines to make her suits not only garments but also heirlooms.

Sam spends most of his time making music and painting. Based on the demands of the month, and whether he has a gallery exhibit or a show, he alternates between these two pursuits as his artistic outlet. Sam lives his craft and grew up in a home where music was always blaring. Today he carries the tradition well, claiming there is "always music in the morning."

Both Sam and Ashley hail from the Pacific Northwest and grew up enjoying serene hometown settings, with verdant plains, mountains to hike, and the occasional bear sighting. Their history has led them to establish their own relaxed gastronomic traditions that make their Brooklyn space feel like a home three thousand miles to the west. •

Spicy Basil Lemon Chicken with Caprese Salad on Crostini

FOR THE CAPRESE AND CROSTINI

½ baguette, cut into 12 to 16 slices

3 tablespoons (45 milliliters) extra-virgin olive oil

1 pound (455 grams) fresh mozzarella, cut into 12 to 16 slices

1½ cups (1½ ounces/45 grams) fresh basil leaves

2 large ripe tomatoes, cut into 12 to 16 slices

Salt and freshly ground black pepper

FOR THE CHICKEN

5 tablespoons (75 milliliters) olive oil

3 garlic cloves, minced

4 boneless, skinless chicken breasts (about 1½ pounds/ 680 grams)

Salt and freshly ground black pepper

1 jalapeño pepper, ribs and seeds removed, minced

2 lemons, ends trimmed and cut into 8 rounds

1 cup (30 grams) fresh basil leaves, chopped

SAM & ASHLEY: *Sundays are usually for puttering around, doing some errands, and organizing what has come undone during the busy week. After things are in order, the moment calls for an easy dish that looks colorful and tastes bright.*

FOR THE CAPRESE AND CROSTINI

Position a rack in the center of the oven and preheat the oven to 425°F (218°C).

Arrange the baguette slices in a single layer on a baking stone or baking sheet. Drizzle the bread with the olive oil and bake for about 8 minutes or until golden and crisp. Transfer to a rack and cool for 5 minutes.

Top each crostino with the mozzarella, basil, and tomatoes, then season with salt and pepper to taste.

FOR THE CHICKEN

Heat ¼ cup (60 milliliters) of the olive oil in a small skillet over medium-low heat until shimmering. Add the garlic and cook, stirring frequently, for about 2 minutes or until soft and fragrant. Remove the skillet from the heat.

Season the chicken breasts with salt and pepper and place them in a large well-seasoned cast-iron skillet. Add the garlic-oil mixture and the jalapeño and turn the chicken twice to coat. Cover the chicken with the lemon slices and drizzle with the remaining 1 tablespoon (15 milliliters) olive oil.

Position a rack in the upper third of the oven and set the oven to broil. Cook the chicken for about 15 minutes or until the temperature registers 160°F (70°C) on an instant-read thermometer. Transfer to a rack and cool for 5 minutes. Sprinkle with the basil and serve with the crostini.

Serves 4

"There was always music playing when I was growing up, always. On weekends we would wake up to music in the kitchen while something was cooking up—something beautiful happening while we were all shaggy-headed and crusty-eyed. The music continued all day. A friend recently told me that it struck him as the funniest thing: 'I came over for dinner, and your dad was cooking with James Brown blaring. We all sat to eat and held hands to pray, and I kept thinking "Who is going over to turn down the stereo?" when suddenly your dad just shouted out over it, "Lord . . ." No one even thought it should be turned down.'"

—SAM OWENS

"We both grew up with copious amounts of apple pie. Instead of asking for birthday cake, Sam would insist on pie instead. My grandma always had an apple pie or two ready for any occasion. As life became busier, apple crisp replaced the more involved pie of yesteryear. A good topping can remind you of a great crust, with half the prep time. We rely on the crisp to remind us of those family moments."

—ASHLEY OWENS

Apple Crisp

FOR THE TOPPING

1 cup (5 ounces/140 grams) unbleached all-purpose flour

⅔ cup (4.6 ounces/130 grams) granulated sugar

⅓ cup (2.6 ounces/75 grams) packed dark brown sugar

½ cup (1¾ ounces/50 grams) quick-cooking oats

¾ teaspoon ground allspice

5 tablespoons (2½ ounces/70 grams) unsalted butter, melted and cooled

FOR THE APPLE LAYER

3 tablespoons (1½ ounces/44 grams) unsalted butter

8 tart apples (about 3 pounds/1.4 kilograms), peeled, cored, and cut into ½-inch (1.3-centimeter) slices

Juice of 2 lemons

¼ cup (1¾ ounces/50 grams) granulated sugar

1 tablespoon (0.3 ounce/9 grams) unbleached all-purpose flour

⅛ teaspoon ground cinnamon

Coarse sea salt

FOR THE TOPPING

Combine the flour, sugars, oats, and allspice in a medium bowl and mix until combined. Add the butter and mix with your fingertips until crumbly. Reserve.

FOR THE APPLE LAYER

Position a rack in the center of the oven and preheat the oven to 375°F (190°C).

Grease an 8-inch (20-centimeter) square baking dish with 2 tablespoons (30 grams) of the butter.

In a large bowl, toss the apple slices with the lemon juice. Combine the sugar, flour, cinnamon, and ½ teaspoon salt in a small bowl, then add to the apples and toss until they're evenly coated. Transfer the apples to the prepared dish, then sprinkle with the reserved topping. Sprinkle the topping with a pinch of salt.

Cover the crisp with a sheet of parchment paper, then with a piece of foil. Cook for 25 minutes or until the apples begin to release their juices. Cut the remaining 1 tablespoon (14 grams) butter into small cubes. Remove the parchment and foil, then sprinkle the crisp with the butter and lightly stir it into the topping to incorporate.

Cook for 30 to 35 minutes or until the crisp is golden. Transfer to a rack and cool for 15 minutes. Serve warm with ice cream, if desired.

Serves 6

CHRISTA FREEMAN & JESS EDDY

{ ICE CREAM MAKERS }

In 2010 Christa Freeman and Jess Eddy, better known, respectively, under the business name Phin & Phebes, found themselves literally neck high in ice cream, which could assumedly be the best place to find yourself. The pair had started making ice cream from their kitchen as a way to pass the frigid winter months. The hobby quickly became more than a fleeting seasonal activity, and soon enough, Christa and Jess were selling their tasty creations in markets and stores across New York City. Full-time jobs were quit, a business plan developed, and ingredient sourcing determined. Phin & Phebes was standing on both legs and running.

By maintaining a strict demand for only the best ingredients, sourcing them locally, and constantly coming up with inventive yet balanced flavors, this young ice cream partnership has taken New York by a sweet storm. Their model is based on the idea that good ice cream comes first from good milk. So, they source from a cooperative of farms from surrounding New York counties, where the milk is so good it wins awards. Then they use that milk to make flavors that are natural, yet still new. Flavors like Vietnamese Coffee, Vanilla Cinnamon, or Coconut Key Lime. As far as flavor combinations go, Christa and Jess are willing to do what it takes to translate delicious flavor pairings into an ice cream—even if that calls for throwing entire chunks of pie into their mixer.

At home and away from the dessert world, Christa and Jess find peace and quiet on slow Saturday mornings, when they can scramble some eggs and lazily watch the early hours pass. During the week, their days are much more rapid. They sneak time to grill in the summer, but otherwise, their dinners have to be fresh, tasty, and fast. These ladies do not have the time for the unnecessary trappings of high-end cooking and entertaining when the world of ice cream is on their shoulders. They opt instead for simple dinners with friends, and shaken cocktails in vintage glassware. That was all right by us. They fed us ice cream, and we enjoyed every minute of their hospitable company. ◆

Hummingbird Cake
with Cream Cheese Frosting

FOR THE CAKE

2 tablespoons (0.6 ounce/
28 grams) unsalted butter, at
room temperature

3¼ cups (16¼ ounces/
460 grams) all-purpose flour

3 bananas

2 cups (14 ounces/400 grams)
sugar

1 teaspoon (3 grams) baking
soda

1 teaspoon (3 grams) ground
cinnamon

1 teaspoon (6 grams) salt

3 large eggs, beaten and at room
temperature

1½ cups (12 ounces/
360 milliliters) vegetable oil

One 8-ounce (227-gram)
can crushed pineapple

1½ teaspoons (7.5 milliliters)
vanilla extract

2¼ cups (9 ounces/255 grams)
pecans, chopped

JESS: *Whenever I dream of cake, this is the one I dream about. My Grana Rogers was known for her baking and this is my mother's favorite cake of hers. Every year my mom bakes this for her close friends on their birthdays.*

FOR THE CAKE

Position two racks in the upper third and lower third of the oven and preheat the oven to 350°F/177°C. Grease three 9-inch/23-centimeter round cake pans with the butter. Dust the pans with ¼ cup/35 grams flour and knock out any excess; set aside.

Finely chop the bananas and measure out 2 cups/340 grams; reserve any leftovers for a different use. In a large bowl, whisk together the remaining 3 cups/425 grams flour, the sugar, baking soda, cinnamon, and salt. Add the eggs and oil and stir just until the dry ingredients are moistened. Stir in the pineapple, vanilla, and half of the pecans.

Divide the batter equally among the prepared pans. Set two pans on the top rack and one on the bottom. Bake, rotating and alternating the cakes halfway through the baking time, for 25 to 30 minutes or until a tester inserted in the center of the cakes comes out clean. Transfer the cakes to racks and cool in the pans for 10 minutes, then invert them directly onto the racks and cool completely, about 1 hour.

FOR THE FROSTING

Two 8-ounce (454 grams) packages cream cheese, at room temperature

2 sticks (8 ounces/227 grams) unsalted butter, at room temperature

2 pounds (908 grams) confectioners' sugar

1 teaspoon (5 milliliters) vanilla extract

FOR THE FROSTING AND ASSEMBLY

While the cake cools, beat the cream cheese and butter with an electric mixer on medium speed until light and fluffy, about 3 minutes. Decrease the speed to low and add the confectioners' sugar and vanilla. Beat until light and fluffy, about 3 minutes.

To assemble, spread the frosting between the layers, scattering some of the remaining pecans in between. Continue spreading the frosting on the top and sides of the cake and sprinkle the remaining pecans on top. Serve.

Pictured on page 64
Serves 10 to 12

SAER RICHARDS

{ BLOGGER }

For those who love to write about food, descriptive energies are often focused on the way the meal tasted, looked, or felt. A former perfume developer, Saer Richards brings a new perspective, courtesy of her finely tuned sense of smell: she connects the wafting aromas of favorite foods to the feelings they evoke, be they comforting or nostalgic.

In Brooklyn, Saer has found a home among the eclectic mix of people and cultures. Living in Brooklyn means never wanting for new experiences, new foods to try, or new people to meet. Her writing,

---

*"To me, hospitality is key to inviting people into your life—to opening yourself up to be inspired by their amazingness. Everyone who passes through my home is offered tea, coffee, cake, dinner, something! It is an invitation not just to be satiated but also to be a part of my life—to be someone who incites me to do good and allows me to do the same for them." —*SAER RICHARDS

---

found in various publications and on her blog, *Craven Maven*, reflects her passion for her neighborhood, her appreciation for a well-made cup of coffee, and her way with words.

Saer invites the reader into her world rather than merely offering a glimpse at her experience through the window of words. This literary magnanimity grew out of her intention to make hospitality not just an occasional gesture in her home but also a way of life. Her conviction came from realizing that all of her great interpersonal experiences began by sharing food or drink. So now when she offers guests tea, cake, or dinner, she says she is not just offering them nourishment but inviting them to be a part of her life. When we were with her in her apartment, her hospitality made us feel we were the most honored of guests in her home. ◆

Sweet Potato–Quinoa Burgers

1 pound (455 grams) sweet
potatoes, scrubbed

½ cup (3½ ounces/100 grams)
quinoa

¼ cup (60 milliliters) olive oil

Kosher salt

1 cup (240 milliliters) water

1 cup (4 ounces/115 grams)
chickpea (besan) flour, plus
additional for dredging

Freshly ground black pepper

1 teaspoon (3 grams) ground
celery seeds

1 teaspoon (3 grams) ground
coriander

1 teaspoon (3 grams) sesame
seeds (optional)

SAER: *I like to prepare the burger mix the day before the burgers are to be consumed.*

Serve on your favorite warm burger bun (I prefer whole wheat bagel thins), with your favorite burger fixings (my choices are arugula or mixed greens, watercress, avocado, homemade ketchup, and a dash of mayo— often double-stacked burger patties with my favorite cheese melted in between).

Position a rack in the center of the oven and preheat the oven to 350°F (177°C).

Arrange the potatoes on a baking sheet and cook them for about 45 minutes or until tender. Transfer the sheet to a rack to cool the potatoes for about 10 minutes.

Meanwhile, rinse the quinoa under cold running water in a fine-mesh sieve until the water runs clear. Heat 1 tablespoon (15 milliliters) of the olive oil in a medium saucepan over medium-high heat until shimmering. Add the quinoa and ½ teaspoon (3 grams) salt and cook, stirring, for about 5 minutes or until the quinoa is beginning to dry and turn golden. Add the water and bring to a boil. Reduce the heat to medium and simmer for about 10 minutes or until most of the water has evaporated. Reduce the heat to low, cover, and cook for about 15 minutes until all of the water has been absorbed and the quinoa is tender. Fluff the quinoa with a fork and transfer to a salad bowl. Cool completely.

Peel the potatoes and mash them in a medium bowl. Mix in the quinoa. Add the chickpea flour ¼ cup (0.75 ounce/22 grams) at a time, stirring well after each addition. The mixture should be tacky but soft. Cover the bowl with plastic wrap and refrigerate overnight.

1 teaspoon (0.63 gram) chopped fresh cilantro

1 teaspoon (0.63 gram) chopped fresh basil

4 ounces (115 grams) green beans

2 baby bok choy (about 10 ounces/280 grams), chopped

2 small shallots, finely chopped

1 garlic clove, crushed

8 hamburger buns or bagels

The next day, fold in 1 teaspoon (3 grams) pepper and the celery seeds, coriander, sesame seeds, cilantro, and basil. Set aside.

Bring a medium saucepan of water to a boil. Add the green beans and blanch for 30 to 60 seconds or until they turn bright green. Drain and run the green beans under cold running water. Chop the green beans; set aside.

Heat 1 tablespoon (15 milliliters) olive oil in a large skillet over medium heat until shimmering. Add the bok choy, shallots, and garlic and cook, stirring, for 5 minutes or until the shallots are soft and translucent. Stir in the green beans, season with salt and pepper, then stir the mixture into the sweet potato mixture.

Using a 1-tablespoon (15-milliliter) measure, scoop out the burger mixture and form patties 3 inches (7.62 centimeters) in diameter. Spread chickpea flour on a plate and coat each patty, shaking off any excess.

Heat the remaining 2 tablespoons (30 milliliters) olive oil in a large skillet over medium heat until beginning to smoke. Cook the burgers for about 3 minutes per side or until well browned. Transfer to a plate and serve two patties in each hamburger bun. Serve with condiments of your choice.

Note: You can coat the patties in sesame seeds instead of chickpea flour.

Pictured on pages 70–71
Serves 8

KARI MORRIS

{ OWNER, MORRIS KITCHEN }

Kari Morris knew she wanted to create something tangible, tasty, well packaged, and useful. She found it in the exemplary syrup that she created alongside her brother, Tyler, an accomplished and passionate chef. What started as a casual ginger syrup became the foundation for Morris Kitchen after it was packaged in nostalgic, apothecary-style jars dressed with a carefully crafted, embossed label.

Over time, the brand has expanded, today including spiced apple syrup, rhubarb syrup, and preserved lemon syrup. The family business continues to grow, with the products currently sold by many retailers around New York City and online through multiple venues. Folks across the world are sampling the Morrises' sweet concoctions and

"The most unusual cooking methods are sometimes the simplest; just knowing the different cutting techniques—for example, dice, julienne, brunoise, and batonnet—and when to use them is invaluable." —KARI MORRIS

finding inventive recipes to showcase them. Although the syrups can be used in all sorts of dishes, Kari showed us how they really shine in cocktails. She shook up glasses of a frothy rum and ginger syrup mixture speckled with sea salt which looked as beautiful as they tasted.

Kari has a background in teaching and facilitating programs about local food and healthy eating habits for both kids and adults. Her passion for the right ingredients—which for her means those sourced locally—paved the way for her career even before Morris Kitchen came about. Her education in art taught her that the cycle of creating, making mistakes, learning from those past attempts, and starting over again is the process from which greatness comes. In teaching, as in cooking, there is no perfect science, but rather a careful art of communicating, experimenting, and expending valiant effort. Kari uses all of her platforms to spread the doctrine of good food eaten together, drizzled with sweet and savory syrups. ◆

Sea Legs

¼ cup (60 milliliters) aged rum

2 tablespoons (30 milliliters)
Morris Kitchen Ginger Syrup

2 tablespoons (30 milliliters)
fresh lime juice

1 large egg white

Ice, chipped

1 ice cube

Coarse sea salt

KARI: *This is a nice cocktail to make when entertaining a few friends.*

Combine the rum, syrup, lime juice, and egg white with some chipped ice and shake until combined, chilled, and frothy. Place the ice cube in a highball glass and strain the cocktail into it. Garnish with coarse sea salt and serve immediately.

Makes 1 drink

Simple Market Vegetable Salad

FOR THE DRESSING

2 tablespoons (30 milliliters) apple cider vinegar

1 tablespoon (15 milliliters) Morris Kitchen Ginger Syrup

1 tablespoon (15 grams) whole-grain mustard

Juice of 1 lemon

2 tablespoons (30 milliliters) olive oil

Sea salt and freshly ground black pepper

FOR THE SALAD

2 teaspoons (10 milliliters) olive oil

½ cup (0.5 ounce/15 grams) walnuts

Sea salt and freshly ground black pepper

Juice of ½ lemon

1 grapefruit

1 fennel bulb

1 head of radicchio

1 red or golden beet, scrubbed and trimmed

½ cup (½ ounce/15 grams) flat-leaf parsley leaves, chopped

Pecorino cheese

FOR THE DRESSING

Whisk the vinegar, syrup, mustard, and lemon juice together in a small bowl. Slowly whisk in the olive oil and whisk until the mixture is emulsified. Season with salt and pepper to taste and refrigerate until needed. Whisk to reincorporate the ingredients before using.

FOR THE SALAD

Heat the olive oil in a small skillet over medium heat until shimmering. Add the walnuts and cook, stirring, for about 5 minutes or until toasted and fragrant. Season with salt and set aside.

Fill a medium bowl with equal parts ice cubes and cold water. Stir in the lemon juice and set aside.

Trim off the top and bottom ends of the grapefruit; the pink flesh should be visible. Set the grapefruit on a cutting board. With a sharp knife, cut the peel and pith off the grapefruit, starting at the top and working down the rounded sides all the way to the bottom. Trim off any pith pieces that may remain. Hold the grapefruit in the palm of your hand over a small bowl and carefully remove the segments by cutting into the flesh toward the center of the grapefruit, using the membranes to guide your cuts. (Alternatively, cut the peeled grapefruit crosswise into slices ¼ inch [0.64 centimeter] thick, then cut the slices in half.) Set aside.

Cut the stalk off the fennel bulb and discard, cut the bulb in half, cut out the tough core, and slice the bulb as thinly as possible on a mandoline (see Note). Place the slices in the prepared acidulated ice bath. Slice the radicchio as thinly as possible on a mandoline and refrigerate it in a salad bowl.

Slice the beet on the mandoline as thinly as possible and toss in the bowl with the vinaigrette.

Remove the fennel from the ice bath, pat it dry with paper towels, and add it to the salad bowl. Add the grapefruit and any accumulated juice and the parsley and toss to combine the ingredients. Season with salt and pepper and divide among four plates. Top the salads with the beets, walnuts, and thin shavings of pecorino cheese. Serve immediately.

Note: A mandoline is the most efficient tool for slicing vegetables paper-thin, as they should be for this recipe. If you don't have one, use a very sharp chef's knife.

Serves 4

RACHEL &
ADAM PATRICK JONES

{ WRITER AND EDITOR/PRODUCER }

The sign of true creatives could be that their work never ends. It pulls them from their sleep at night and tugs at them during the workday. Rachel and Adam Patrick Jones are no exception. They live their days in challenging, creative work environments—Rachel at an advertising agency, Adam as a freelance editor/producer—and still return to their Brooklyn home in the evenings ready to feed the creative beast. The two are the quiet inspiration and leadership behind the website

"I grew up in a family of six where we were expected to eat every meal (school or sports permitting) together. That means that I've spent nearly thirteen thousand meals sitting at the dining table in conversation with my parents and siblings. Sunday roast beef has been paired with arguments, stir-fry has been peppered with political discussions, and dessert has often ended in tears. But I would have it no other way." —RACHEL JONES

Industry of One, which operates as a blog but serves as an archive and looks like a periodical. Its mission is to profile individuals who are working hard and doing it with style, sartorial and otherwise. Each post is a visual map of a unique personality enhanced by illuminating background and a probing interview. Visitors to the site come away with insights they can use and inspiration to keep cultivating their own style.

Rachel and Adam are documenting a generation of young people who demonstrate that putting in a hard day's work, day after day, in any industry or business entity, does not have to mean sacrificing individuality to the perilous anonymity of "business casual." In fact it can mean finding a way to enhance the endeavors of the field you work in through your own carefully crafted image. These two live their vision. Though they each work tirelessly, they also value everyday pleasures, like drinking americanos and soy chai lattes on their brownstone's steps, and familial ones, such as long Sunday night roast beef dinners. Rachel and Adam have found the style that fits their personalities and their industries, and are showing all of us how others wear theirs. ◆

Tortilla Española

2¼ cups (18 ounces/
540 milliliters) olive oil

1 yellow onion, chopped

Salt

2 large russet potatoes, thinly
sliced on a mandoline (see
Note)

3 large eggs

Heat 2 tablespoons (30 milliliters) of the olive oil in a large skillet
over medium-high heat until shimmering. Add the onion and a
pinch of salt and cook, stirring, for about 5 minutes or until soft and
translucent. Transfer the onion to a bowl; reserve.

Heat an additional 2 cups (480 milliliters) of the olive oil over
medium heat until shimmering. Add the potatoes to the skillet and
cook for 15 to 20 minutes or until the potatoes are soft and light
golden. Remove the skillet from the heat.

In a large bowl, beat the eggs and 1½ teaspoons (0.3 ounce/
9 grams) salt and stir in the cooked onion. One spoonful at a time,
add the potatoes, along with the cooking oil, stirring after each
addition.

Scrape any potato bits out of the skillet. Heat the remaining
2 tablespoons (30 milliliters) olive oil in the empty skillet over
medium heat until shimmering. Add the egg-potato mixture to the
skillet: do not stir. Cook for about 6 minutes or until the bottom of
the tortilla has set. Slide a fork underneath the tortilla to check for
doneness—it should be golden and come away from the skillet easily.

Remove the skillet from the heat. With the help of a spatula, slide
the tortilla onto a large plate (the plate should be larger than the
tortilla). Drain and discard the excess oil. Using dish towels or oven
mitts, invert the skillet over the plate, hold the plate and skillet
together (they should close like a clamshell), and invert the plate to
return the tortilla, cooked side up, to the skillet. Cook the tortilla
over medium heat for 3 to 4 minutes or until it is completely set.

Allow the tortilla to cool in the skillet for 10 to 15 minutes, then cut
into wedges and serve warm or at room temperature. The tortilla is
best the day it is made.

Note: A mandoline is the most efficient tool for slicing the potatoes
paper-thin, as they should be for this recipe. If you don't have one,
use a very sharp chef's knife.

Pictured on page 82
Serves 4 to 6

Chocolate Chip Zucchini Cake

Nonstick baking spray

2½ cups (12½ ounces/ 355 grams) all-purpose flour

¼ cup (0.75 ounce/21 grams) natural cocoa powder

1 teaspoon (3 grams) baking soda

½ teaspoon baking powder

½ teaspoon ground cinnamon

½ teaspoon ground cloves

½ cup (4 ounces/115 grams) margarine, at room temperature

½ cup (120 milliliters) vegetable oil

1¾ cups (12¼ ounces/ 347 grams) sugar

2 large eggs, at room temperature

½ cup (120 milliliters) sour milk or buttermilk

1 teaspoon (5 milliliters) vanilla extract

Approximately 2 cups (12 ounces/340 grams) zucchini, finely diced

½ cup (6 ounces/170 grams) semisweet chocolate chips

RACHEL: *I always feel slightly abashed about telling visitors the name of this dish. I have the inkling that a former five-year-old self still lurks inside all of us and will inevitably roar to life at the mention of zucchini for dessert. "Zucchini, you say? I'm still full from dinner." In the case of this well-worn family favorite, zucchini is the stellar ingredient that elevates this simple Betty Crocker–esque chocolate cake from ho-hum to amazing. It steals the scene from the chocolate (which in my book is unheard of). I'm not sure where along the way this dish weaseled itself into my family's go-to recipe list, but I'm always surprised that more people haven't heard of it. It's that good. And can I say simple?*

Position a rack in the center of the oven and preheat the oven to 325°F (162°C). Generously coat the inside of a 13-by-9-inch (33-by-23-centimeter) baking pan with nonstick baking spray.

Combine the flour, cocoa, baking soda, baking powder, cinnamon, and cloves in a medium bowl; set aside.

Beat the margarine, oil, and sugar in a mixing bowl with an electric mixer on medium speed until smooth, about 3 minutes. Add the eggs one at a time, beating well after each addition. Add the sour milk and vanilla and beat until just combined.

Reduce the mixer speed to low, add half of the flour mixture, and mix for 15 seconds. Add the remaining flour mixture and beat just until incorporated. Scrape down the sides of the bowl, then beat for 5 more seconds.

Stir in the zucchini and half of the chocolate chips. Scrape the batter into the prepared pan and sprinkle the top with the remaining chocolate chips.

Bake for 35 to 40 minutes or until a tester inserted in the center of the cake comes out clean. Transfer the cake to a rack and cool completely in the pan, about 1 hour. Serve with vanilla ice cream.

Pictured on page 83
Serves 12

DIANA YEN

{ FOOD STYLIST/CATERER }

The Jewels of New York are a true gem in the energetic and creatively bustling Big Apple. This small band of culinary enthusiasts comprises a multidisciplinary creative studio using food as its medium. Both sophisticated and knowledgeable, the Jewels aim to make food experiences inviting and homey for every client. Through catering, food styling, and food consultation services, the Jewels of New York are reinventing food as art—delicious, edible, make-you-feel-good art. No one more clearly embodies the vision of the Jewels than its visionary leader, Diana Yen.

A resident of Brooklyn Heights, Diana has a professional background in home and lifestyle design, which perhaps follows

"I believe in following the seasons and like to eat the freshest things around me, but I also think that being extreme in any diet can limit you from trying other foods. Food is about living, so it's important to keep those doors open and let your taste buds explore." —DIANA YEN

naturally for a person who has held a lifelong interest in food and gravitates toward being a homebody. She grew up eating nightly home-cooked dinners, and afternoon snacks always awaited her when she got off the school bus. Diana was raised in an environment where she learned to enjoy and cherish food, a gift she attributes to her mother. Nowadays Diana not only runs the Jewels of New York but also cooks meals for all who come to her home. In a city that is more accustomed to on-the-fly takeout, cooking is her way of slowing down and nourishing both herself and her community.

What has come to be the Jewels of New York is a natural outgrowth of Diana's warm, imaginative personality, which manifests itself in the creation of artful, thoughtful food. *(On pages 91 and 92 Diana is photographed with her assistant Hannah Schmitz.)* ◆

Ginger Ice Cream
with Kumquat Compote

FOR THE ICE CREAM

1 cup (12 ounces/340 grams) fresh ginger, peeled and coarsely grated

1 cup plus 2 tablespoons (7½ ounces/225 grams) sugar

3 cups (720 milliliters) whole milk

2 cups (480 milliliters) heavy cream

1 vanilla bean

3 large egg yolks

FOR THE ICE CREAM

Place the ginger in a large, heavy saucepan and add enough cold water to cover it by 1 inch (2.5 centimeters). Bring to a boil over medium-high heat, then reduce the heat to medium-low and simmer for 5 minutes. Drain the ginger and discard the liquid.

Return the ginger to the saucepan and stir in the sugar, milk, and cream. Split the vanilla bean in half lengthwise and scrape the seeds into the pan, discarding the pods (or put them in a bowl of sugar to make vanilla sugar). Bring the mixture to a simmer over medium heat.

Meanwhile, whisk the egg yolks in a large heatproof bowl until they turn pale in color. Wrap a damp towel around the base of the bowl to keep it steady. In a very slow, steady stream, whisk in about ¼ cup (60 milliliters) of the simmering ginger-cream mixture. Slowly and steadily pour in the remaining mixture, whisking constantly.

Return the mixture to the saucepan and cook, stirring constantly, over medium-low heat for 7 to 10 minutes, never allowing the mixture to come to a boil, until it is thick enough to coat the back of a spoon. Remove the saucepan from the heat and allow the mixture to steep for 30 minutes. Strain the mixture into a large bowl through a fine-mesh strainer and discard the solids. Cover the bowl with plastic wrap and refrigerate until the mixture is completely chilled, at least 2 hours. The ice cream base may be prepared up to 2 days in advance.

Churn the mixture in an ice cream maker according to the manufacturer's instructions, then transfer it to a 1-quart (960-milliliter) container and freeze until firm, at least 2 hours. Ice cream is best when served within 2 days of making (homemade ice cream tends to become icier than store-bought).

FOR THE COMPOTE

1 cup (7 ounces/200 grams) sugar

1 cup (240 milliliters) water

1 pound (455 grams) kumquats, scrubbed, halved, and seeded

2 star anise pods

2 cardamom pods

Two ½-inch (1.28-centimeter) slices fresh ginger

FOR THE COMPOTE

Stir the sugar and water together in a large, heavy saucepan. Bring the mixture to a boil over medium-high heat, stirring until the sugar is completely dissolved. Stir in the kumquats, star anise, cardamom, and ginger and return the mixture to a boil. Reduce the heat to medium and simmer for about 30 minutes or until thickened and jamlike. Transfer the compote to three 8-ounce (237-milliliter) jars with tight-fitting lids. Kumquat compote can be made up to 3 days in advance and stored, refrigerated, in an airtight container.

Serve the ice cream with the compote.

Pictured on page 90
Makes about 1 quart/1 liter of ice cream;
16 to 24 ounces/475 to 710 milliliters of compote

"I love unplanned late-night meals with friends. They usually come after many drinks and going out, and there's a warm buzz that comes from being with your favorite people and talking, even if it's over simple diner food."

—DIANA YEN

Salmon Ochazuke (Tea-Poached Salmon with Brown Rice)

DIANA: *The traditional recipe for* ochazuke *calls for matcha green tea, but we loved the floral aroma and golden broth that jasmine tea created. The fattiness of the salmon lends itself to a rich and round-flavored broth. You can use leftover rice for this recipe.*

FOR THE RICE

1 cup (7 ounces/200 grams) short-grain brown rice

Pinch of kosher salt

FOR THE SALMON

4 cups (960 milliliters) hot water

1 teaspoon dashi powder

1 pound (455 grams) salmon, cut into 4 fillets ¾ inch (1.9 centimeters) thick and skinned

Kosher salt

4 cups (960 milliliters) brewed jasmine, genmaicha, or matcha tea

4 umeboshi plums

Nori, cut into strips

FOR THE RICE

Rinse the rice under cold running water in a fine-mesh sieve until the water runs clear. Combine the rice, 2 cups (480 milliliters) water, and a pinch of salt in a medium saucepan and bring to a boil over medium-high heat. Reduce the heat to low, cover, and cook for 45 to 60 minutes or until the rice is tender and all the water has been absorbed. Remove the rice from the heat and allow it to rest for 10 minutes, then fluff it with a fork.

FOR THE SALMON

Combine the hot water and dashi powder and stir until the powder is dissolved. Rub the salmon fillets with 1½ tablespoons (25 grams) salt. Allow the salmon to rest at room temperature for 10 minutes.

Meanwhile, bring the tea and dashi stock to a simmer over medium heat in a medium saucepan. Mound a quarter of the rice in each of four shallow bowls, then top each one with a plum. Wipe the salt off the salmon and arrange one fillet over each plum-topped rice mound.

Ladle the simmering broth over the salmon and allow the salmon to poach for 2 to 3 minutes or until it reaches the desired doneness. Garnish each dish with sliced nori and serve.

Serves 4

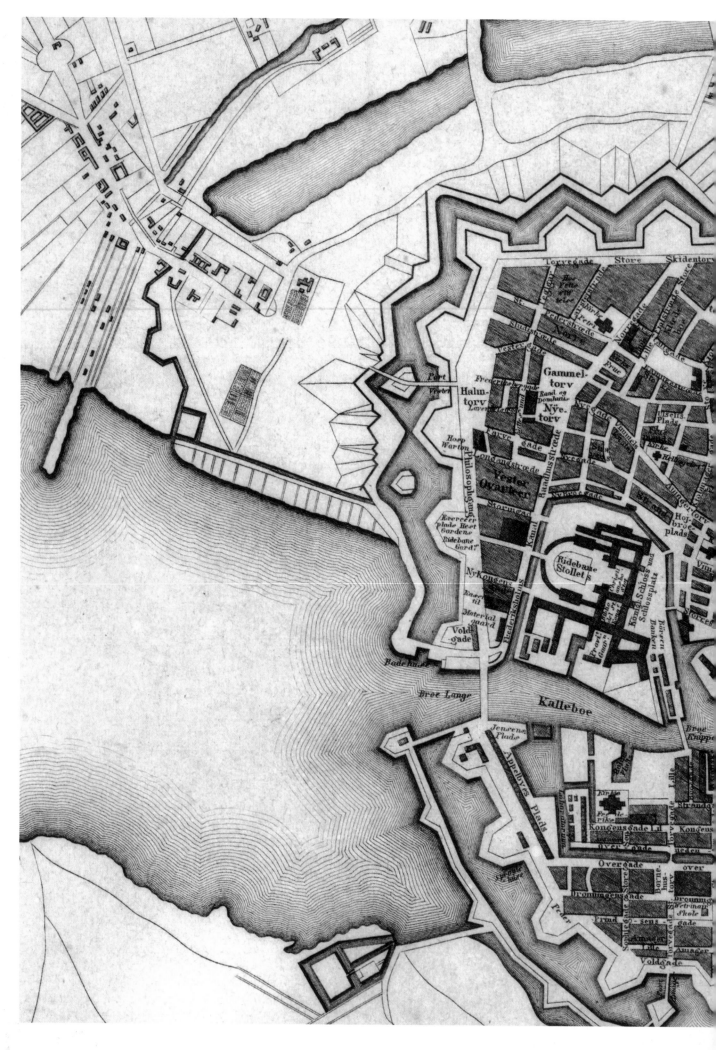

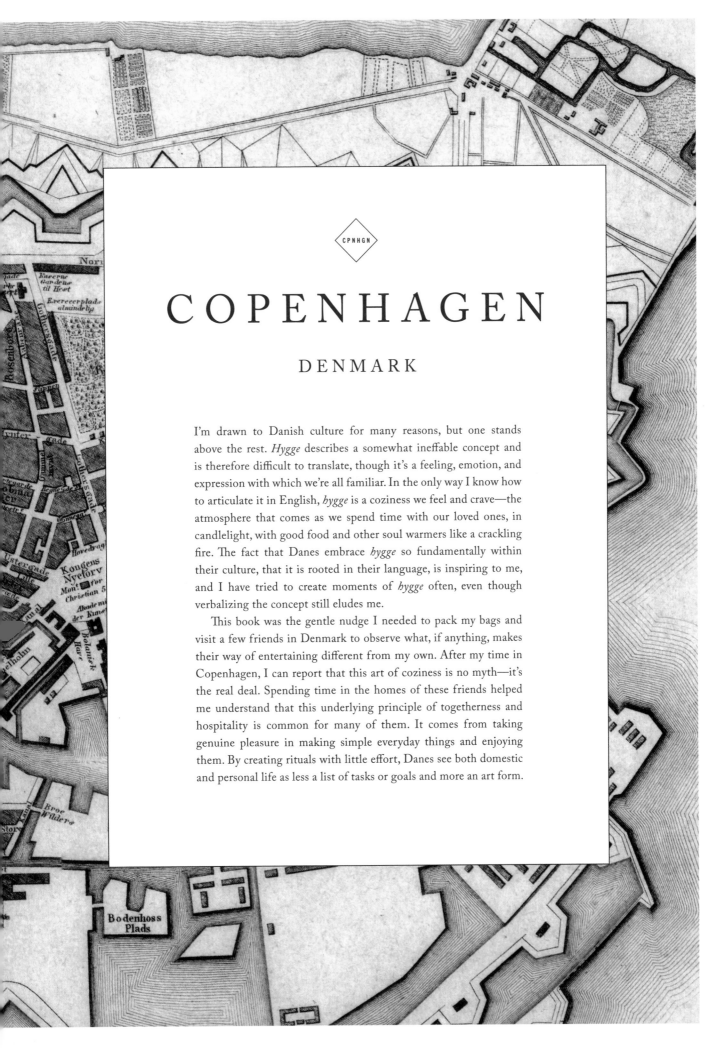

COPENHAGEN

DENMARK

I'm drawn to Danish culture for many reasons, but one stands above the rest. *Hygge* describes a somewhat ineffable concept and is therefore difficult to translate, though it's a feeling, emotion, and expression with which we're all familiar. In the only way I know how to articulate it in English, *hygge* is a coziness we feel and crave—the atmosphere that comes as we spend time with our loved ones, in candlelight, with good food and other soul warmers like a crackling fire. The fact that Danes embrace *hygge* so fundamentally within their culture, that it is rooted in their language, is inspiring to me, and I have tried to create moments of *hygge* often, even though verbalizing the concept still eludes me.

This book was the gentle nudge I needed to pack my bags and visit a few friends in Denmark to observe what, if anything, makes their way of entertaining different from my own. After my time in Copenhagen, I can report that this art of coziness is no myth—it's the real deal. Spending time in the homes of these friends helped me understand that this underlying principle of togetherness and hospitality is common for many of them. It comes from taking genuine pleasure in making simple everyday things and enjoying them. By creating rituals with little effort, Danes see both domestic and personal life as less a list of tasks or goals and more an art form.

MIKKEL LIPPMANN

{ ADVERTISING EXECUTIVE }

Weekly multigenerational family meals are a rarity on any continent, and Europe is no exception. Mikkel Lippmann's family has, however, decided not to let general busyness, ballet practices, or work interfere with their common priority: Tuesday night dinners with the entire family—three generations, from granddaughters to grandmothers. It is a weekly point of connection where everyone in the family is involved and present at the table, in the kitchen, and in the dialogue.

Mikkel, an accomplished advertising executive, is also a devoted family man. He is husband to the creative and beautiful Malene and father to Olga and Olivia. Mikkel's mother, Puk, a renowned textile artist, is also at the table, enchanting us with stories of travels and interesting friends. The legacy of creative ambition that characterizes this family is fostered among them over these weeknight dinners and other parties. The Lippmanns reveal purpose-filled lives through their relationships with one another and through the quality of their individual work.

For a family with so many places to be, the meal must be quick, but it must be good. The girls set the table and light the candles. Puk opens a bottle of wine as we nibble on olives and cheeses in the kitchen. Mikkel drizzles fresh vegetables with fine oils and herbs and dresses a long salmon fillet with peppercorns, olive oil, and lemon slices. Malene pulls a thin, sugary apple sheet cake out of the oven, and dinner is ready. Everyone was involved, and everyone will enjoy the fruit of the shared family work—a habit through which the Lippmann clan stands firm. ◆

Cucumber and Fennel Salad

1 large fennel bulb

1 to 2 medium cucumbers, thinly sliced

Grated zest and juice of 1 lemon

Olive oil

Salt and freshly ground black pepper

Cut the tops of the stalks off the fennel bulb and discard. Trim off the fronds and reserve. Finely chop the stalks. Cut the fennel bulb in half, cut out the tough core, and finely slice the bulb; toss the fronds, chopped stalks, and sliced bulb in a large bowl. Add the cucumbers and lemon zest, drizzle with the olive oil and lemon juice, and season with salt and pepper. Toss to combine, and refrigerate for 10 minutes before serving.

Serves 4

Spidskål (Cabbage Salad)

½ cup (2½ ounces/70 grams) sesame seeds

1 medium head green cabbage

Salt and freshly ground black pepper

3 tablespoons (45 milliliters) red wine vinegar

2 teaspoons (10 grams) Dijon mustard

½ cup (120 milliliters) olive oil

Toast the sesame seeds in a medium skillet over medium heat, stirring constantly, until light golden, about 5 minutes.

Remove and discard as many damaged leaves from the exterior of the cabbage as necessary. Cut the cabbage in half and remove and discard the core. Finely chop the cabbage and place it in a large bowl; season with salt and pepper.

Whisk the vinegar and mustard together in a medium bowl. While whisking steadily, drizzle in the olive oil. Season with salt and pepper and drizzle over the cabbage. Toss to coat. Add the sesame seeds and toss to coat once again. Serve.

Serves 6

AUSTIN & ASHLYN SAILSBURY

{ WRITER/CREATIVE CONSULTANT AND TEACHER }

Austin and Ashlyn Sailsbury are newlyweds committed to an adventurous life. In their first tender months of marriage, they uprooted themselves from their familiar home and family life in the southern United States for a new life in a small suburban town outside Copenhagen. Austin, a staff member of an international church, and Ashlyn, a primary school teacher, are learning to make a home out of community and service and shared experiences.

With effortless style and copious candles, they fit well within the landscape of Danes. However, their American Southernness cannot be hidden. The occasional drawl and the aroma of Ashlyn's sweet potato biscuits give them away. They carry with them the best of their native culture: an appreciation for food that warms the soul, and hospitality that puts even the most anxious spirits to rest. And so it is, even in this foreign land, that Austin and Ashlyn abound with energy, humor, and vitality.

Their life in an idyllic town is full of pleasant routines and nights spent cooking together. Following Danish traditions, they light candles when they make their coffee in the morning and again when they come home after work. They plan special Sunday meals together and always invite friends, new and old, to partake. Their marriage is both inwardly focused and outwardly serving. They tend to each other with their words and their actions, yet they also bring others in, making friends and acquaintances feel more loved, more accepted, and more engaged. Though Austin and Ashlyn are young in years and marriage, they are a formidable force for hospitality worldwide. ◆

Pumpkin Bread with Maple-Cinnamon Glaze and Nuts

FOR THE BREAD

4 tablespoons (2 ounces/ 60 grams) unsalted butter

½ cup (120 milliliters) milk

2¼ teaspoons (¼ ounce/ 7.5 grams) active dry yeast

1¼ cups (8¾ ounces/250 grams) sugar

¾ cup (6 ounces/170 grams) pumpkin puree

1 teaspoon (6 grams) salt

2½ cups (15 ounces/425 grams) bread flour

2 tablespoons (30 milliliters) olive oil

2 teaspoons (0.2 ounce/6 grams) ground cinnamon

½ teaspoon freshly grated nutmeg

FOR THE BREAD

In a small saucepan over medium heat, cook 2 tablespoons (30 grams) of the butter, without stirring, until brown bits are visible at the bottom of the pan, 2 to 4 minutes. Stir in the milk and warm it to 110°F (43°C). Transfer the mixture to a large bowl and stir in the yeast and ¼ cup (50 grams) of the sugar. Allow the mixture to stand until it foams, about 10 minutes.

Stir in the pumpkin purée, salt, and 1 cup (170 grams) of the flour. When combined, add the rest of the flour in several additions, kneading between additions. Knead the dough until it is elastic and slightly sticky, 6 to 8 minutes.

Brush a large bowl with the olive oil. Place the dough inside and turn it over several times until it is well greased. Cover the bowl tightly with plastic wrap and allow the dough to rise in a warm, draft-free place until doubled in size, about 1½ hours.

Meanwhile, combine the remaining 1 cup (200 grams) sugar, the cinnamon, the nutmeg, and the remaining 2 tablespoons (30 grams) butter and stir well.

After the dough has doubled in size, knead it for about 2 minutes, then roll it out into a 12-by-9-inch (30-by-23-centimeter) rectangle. Sprinkle it with the sugar mixture, pressing it gently into the dough.

Cut the dough lengthwise into 6 strips, then stack them together. Cut the strips into 6 squares and stack them into a 9-by-5-inch (23-by-13-centimeter) loaf pan. Cover the pan with a clean dish towel, and allow it to rise in a warm, draft-free place until it doubles in size, about 30 minutes.

Position a rack in the center of the oven and preheat the oven to 350°F (177°C). Bake for 30 to 35 minutes or until golden. Transfer the pan to a rack and allow the bread to rest for 5 minutes. Meanwhile, prepare the glaze.

FOR THE MAPLE-
CINNAMON GLAZE

¾ cup (3 ounces/90 grams)
confectioners' sugar

2½ tablespoons (37.5 milliliters)
pure maple syrup

1 tablespoon (0.5 ounce/
15 grams) unsalted butter,
melted

1 to 2 tablespoons (15 to
30 milliliters) milk

¾ cup (3 ounces/90 grams)
roasted and salted pecans,
chopped

FOR THE GLAZE AND NUT TOPPING

In a medium bowl, whisk together the confectioners' sugar,
syrup, butter, and 1 tablespoon (15 milliliters) of the milk. Whisk
in another tablespoon of milk as needed to adjust the consistency
as desired.

Drizzle the glaze over the bread and sprinkle with the pecans. Serve
warm.

Makes 1 loaf

Sweet Potato Biscuits

1 sweet potato (about
11 ounces/310 grams),
peeled and cut into 1-inch
(25-centimeter) pieces

1¾ cups (8¾ ounces/250 grams)
all-purpose flour, plus additional
for dusting

2 tablespoons (30 grams) sugar

2½ teaspoons (0.26 ounce/
7.5 grams) baking powder

1 teaspoon (6 grams) salt

½ teaspoon baking soda

6 tablespoons (3 ounces/
85 grams) unsalted butter, cut
into small pieces and chilled

⅓ cup (80 milliliters)
buttermilk, chilled

Position a rack in the center of the oven and preheat the oven to
425°F (218°C). Line a baking sheet with parchment paper.

Place the sweet potato pieces in a small saucepan and add enough
cold water to cover by about 1 inch (2.5 centimeters). Bring to a boil
over medium-high heat, then reduce the heat to medium. Simmer
for about 10 minutes or until the sweet potatoes are tender.

Drain, then mash the sweet potato until very smooth. Cool to room
temperature and measure out ¾ cup (180 grams). Reserve leftovers
for another use. (The sweet potato puree may be prepared one day in
advance and refrigerated in an airtight container.)

Whisk the flour, sugar, baking powder, salt, and baking soda in a
large bowl. Using two knives, cut the butter into the flour mixture
until it resembles small peas.

Mix the buttermilk and sweet potato puree in a small bowl, then add
it to the flour-butter mixture, stirring just until the ingredients come
together.

Lightly dust a clean, dry work surface with flour. Turn the dough
out and knead it just until combined. With a floured rolling pin,
roll it out into a 12-inch (30-centimeter) circle. Flour a 2½-inch
(6-centimeter) round biscuit cutter, stamp out the biscuits, and
arrange them about 1 inch (2.5 centimeters) apart on the prepared
sheet.

Bake the biscuits for 10 to 12 minutes or until golden. Transfer to a
rack and cool for about 5 minutes. Serve warm.

Makes 12 biscuits

NATHALIE SCHWER

{ INTERIOR DESIGNER }

Nathalie Schwer is the face of young Copenhagen artistry. An accomplished interior designer, a frequent traveler, and a bike commuter, Nathalie embodies the ideals of the rising Danish generation, a generation looking to establish new traditions, further creative strides, and prove to the whole world that the Danish people have a voice to share and a voice worth listening to.

Nathalie's sanctuary is a spacious apartment overlooking Copenhagen's canal. Her rooms are light and airy, brimming with art books and vintage furniture. Her kitchen, filled with the fragrance of fresh rosemary and basil and with sun, provides room enough to gather friends around a sprawling tableful of roasted vegetables and wine.

Like many young Danes, Nathalie eschews archaic traditions. But she holds steadfast to the tenets of cooking with the season, grocery shopping daily, and making meals in the home. "I come from a great number of willful people," she told us while slicing avocados, adding that crafting "homemade food with a variety of fresh ingredients is the healthiest thing you can do."

Nathalie's experience and education in the kitchen began when she was a young child, helping her mother prepare meals or just setting the table. A lifelong contributor to the process, today she cooks with an easy passion and is always ready to host another party or jump on a plane to Paris. She is Copenhagen with curls and Chuck Taylors, a lover of food, people, and sartorial excursions, rooted in the past yet always looking toward the future. •

Hearty Barley Salad with Broiled Feta and Tomatoes

8 ounces (230 grams) feta cheese, cut into ¼-inch (0.64-centimeter) cubes

1½ cups (about 8 ounces/ 230 grams) small ripe tomatoes, such as San Marzano, halved

½ cup (about 2½ ounces/ 70 grams) pitted black olives, halved

¼ cup (0.4 ounce/10 grams) chopped fresh herbs such as oregano, rosemary, and thyme

¼ cup (60 milliliters) extra-virgin olive oil

1 cup (7 ounces/200 grams) pearled barley

2 cups (475 milliliters) water

Salt

2 ripe avocados, cut into ½-inch (1.28-centimeter) cubes

16 ounces (455 grams) marinated artichokes, cut into wedges ½ inch (1.28 centimeters) thick

1 cucumber (about 8 ounces/ 230 grams), seeded and chopped

2 cups (2 ounces/60 grams) fresh basil leaves, thinly sliced

2 tablespoons (30 milliliters) fresh lemon juice

Freshly ground black pepper

NATHALIE: *The melted feta mixture serves as a hearty sauce for this salad. Feel free to customize it with whatever vegetables or herbs you like. Serve it warm with some good bread, maybe some charcuterie, and good red wine.*

Position a rack in the center of the oven and preheat the oven to 392°F (200°C).

Combine the feta, tomatoes, olives, herbs, and olive oil on a foil-lined baking sheet and toss until well mixed. Bake the mixture for about 25 minutes or until the feta has melted and the tomatoes are soft and brown.

Meanwhile, bring the barley, water, and ½ teaspoon salt to a boil in a medium saucepan over medium-high heat. Reduce the heat to medium, cover, and simmer the barley for about 20 minutes or until it is tender. Fluff it with a fork and transfer it to a salad bowl.

Add the avocados, artichokes, cucumber, basil, and lemon juice to the barley and toss to combine. Stir in the feta mixture. Season to taste with salt and pepper. Serve.

Pictured on page 112
Serves 4

MIKKEL &
YUKARI GRØNNEBÆK

{ CURATOR/MENSWEAR DESIGNER
AND FURNITURE DESIGNER }

Just outside the hubbub and chaos of Copenhagen's city center dwell the talented Mikkel and Yukari Grønnebæk, and their sweet baby, Kai. Mikkel, an art gallery curator and cofounder of the menswear line Norse Projects, and his wife, Yukari, a furniture designer originally from Japan, are an artistic power couple. Yet the two greet dinner guests in aprons and house shoes, a casual and disarming welcome.

A long dining room table is the center of their home and symbolically the center of their family life. The two cook together often, as evidenced by their patterned weaving and dancing around their stove and cutting boards and also by their food, which, much like their home, is a beautiful and pure collaboration of their respective Danish and Japanese traditions. This is a home where boiled potatoes with dill are served alongside duck over sticky rice with fiery hints of wasabi. Their styles and tastes do not clash but instead have created an altogether unique and seamless new palate.

As their young son coos to sleep in the corner of the room, the table is abundantly set, plentiful in food and company. The stories and meal, both hearty in nature, make the hours around the table pass quickly. It is here that Mikkel and Yukari, in their artistry, have created something sacred and special, a slow and intimate family place that serves as a refuge from the outside world. ◆

Duck on Japanese Rice with Fresh Danish Green Peas and Wasabi Mayo

1 cup (7 ounces/200 grams) Japanese sticky rice

2 cups (480 milliliters) water

1 piece kombu (optional)

Salt and freshly ground black pepper

1 cup plus 2 tablespoons (10½ ounces/300 grams) Danish green peas, shelled

One 12-ounce (345-gram) duck breast

6 green onions or scallions, thinly sliced

1 fresh chile, such as bird's eye, thinly sliced

Kewpie Japanese mayonnaise

Wasabi paste

MIKKEL & YUKARI: *As a Danish/Japanese couple, we often mix the two cuisines when cooking. A favorite is this simple and easy course with a European/Japanese flavor.*

Rinse the rice under cold running water in a fine-mesh sieve until the water runs clear. Combine the rice, water, and kombu, if using, in a medium saucepan and bring to a boil over medium-high heat. Reduce the heat to low, cover, and cook for 45 to 60 minutes or until the rice is tender and all the water has been absorbed. Remove the rice from the heat and allow it to rest for 10 minutes, then fluff it with a fork. Reserve.

Bring a small saucepan of water to a boil over medium-high heat. Fill a bowl with an equal amount of ice cubes and cold water. Add 1½ teaspoons (3 grams) salt and the peas and cook for about 3 minutes or until bright green. Drain the peas and reserve.

Score the fatty side of the duck breast with a very sharp knife in a crosshatch pattern, being careful not to cut all the way through to the meat. Season with salt and pepper.

Cook the duck, fat side down, in a medium skillet over low heat for about 5 minutes or until the fat begins to render. Remove the duck from the pan, then heat the fat over medium-high heat until shimmering. Return the duck, fat side down, to the skillet and cook for 6 to 8 minutes or until the skin is crisp and golden. Turn the duck and continue cooking for 3 to 4 minutes or until cooked to the desired doneness. Allow the duck to rest on a cutting board for 5 minutes, then thinly slice it.

Toss the rice and peas together and divide between two bowls. Top with the sliced duck, then sprinkle with the green onions and chile. In a small bowl, combine the mayonnaise and wasabi to taste and dollop it on top of the duck. Serve.

Note: You can fill a small plastic bag with the wasabi mayonnaise, cut a very small hole in one corner, and squeeze the mayonnaise onto the dish in a decorative pattern.

Serves 2

COPENHAGEN, DENMARK

SARAH BRITTON

{ HOLISTIC NUTRITIONIST/VEGETARIAN CHEF }

Sarah Britton glows. Whether her brightness is a result of her exceptional whole-food diet or her raw optimism, she empowers people, through both her virtual and physical presence, to take the role of food in their lives seriously. Not as another banality or obligation but because, as she says, food is "so much more than sustenance—it's poetry."

Originally from Toronto, Sarah is a transplant to Copenhagen, though she seems to be a natural in the Scandinavian landscape, thanks to her bike, bohemian style, and perfect topknot. Known for her award-winning blog *My New Roots*, she is a holistic nutritionist and vegetarian chef who reminds students, clients, and blog followers that eating healthfully is the first step in feeling healthy.

"A few years ago I started taking a moment before I eat to give thanks. I wouldn't consider this prayer, or even a religious thing, simply a way to slow down and feel gratitude for the food in front of me. Funnily enough, this little habit has caught on among my family and many friends, who now enjoy a little pause of appreciation before eating, too. Many of them have told me what a significant difference these ten seconds have made in their life, and how much more they consciously enjoy their food." —SARAH BRITTON

Sarah's first food "awakening" occurred when she worked on an organic farm in Arizona. She came to understand natural foods by witnessing how they are grown and harvested organically. The next piece of the puzzle was going back to school to learn how that food interacts, changes, and helps or hinders our bodies.

Sarah is a patient guide in the study of food, what it is, and how it works on our behalf. She talks to us as she mixes ingredients and sifts through ginger powder. We learn that powdered ginger is better for our cells than solid, and that a cup of hot water with lemon is the best thing to drink the moment you wake up. She encourages us all to take healthy eating one step at a time, one step that suits our lives and our tastes. ◆

Four Corners Lentil Stew with Sesame Rice

FOR THE LENTILS

1 cup (6½ ounces/185 grams) red lentils, picked over

2 tablespoons (30 milliliters) coconut oil or ghee

1 large onion, finely chopped

1 teaspoon (6 grams) salt

5 garlic cloves, minced

1 tablespoon (0.45 ounce/13 grams) minced fresh ginger

1 tablespoon (0.14 ounce/4 grams) ground cumin

¼ teaspoon cayenne

One 15-ounce (425-gram) can plum tomatoes, chopped

1 lemon, sliced into rounds

3 cups (700 milliliters) vegetable stock

Chopped fresh cilantro, scallions, or flat-leaf parsley for garnish

FOR THE RICE

1 cup (7 ounces/200 grams) short-grain brown rice

2½ cups (600 milliliters) water

¾ teaspoon salt

¼ cup (1¼ ounces/35 grams) sesame seeds

FOR THE LENTILS

Rinse the lentils under cold running water in a fine-mesh sieve until the water runs clear.

Heat the oil in a medium saucepan over medium-high heat until shimmering. Add the onion and salt and cook, stirring, until it is soft and translucent, about 5 minutes. Add the garlic, ginger, cumin, and cayenne and cook until fragrant, 1 minute. Stir in the tomatoes, three of the lemon slices, the stock, and the lentils.

Bring the mixture to a boil, then reduce the heat to medium-low, cover, and simmer for 20 to 30 minutes or until the lentils are tender.

FOR THE RICE AND SERVING

Rinse the rice under cold running water in a fine-mesh sieve until the water runs clear. Combine the rice, water, and salt in a small saucepan and bring to a boil over medium-high heat. Reduce the heat to low, cover, and cook for 45 to 60 minutes or until the rice is tender and all the water has been absorbed. Remove the rice from the heat and allow it to rest for 10 minutes, then fluff it with a fork.

While the rice cooks, toast the sesame seeds over medium heat in a small skillet, stirring constantly, for about 5 minutes until light golden. Fold the sesame seeds into the rice.

Squeeze the remaining lemon slices over the stew and season with salt to taste. Serve the stew over the sesame rice and sprinkle it with the garnish.

Notes: The onion may be replaced with thinly sliced leeks (white parts only).

Four large ripe tomatoes can be substituted for the canned plum tomatoes.

Serves 4

Spiced Raw Chocolate Mousse

¼ cup (1 ounce/30 grams) hemp seeds (see Note)

2 heaping tablespoons (0.4 ounce/11 grams) raw cacao powder

1 ripe avocado, peeled and pitted

1 large banana, frozen and coarsely chopped

2 tablespoons (1½ ounces/ 42 grams) raw honey, agave, or pure maple syrup

Pinch of cayenne

Pinch of ground ginger

Pinch of sea salt

Cold water, as needed

Blend the hemp seeds, cacao, avocado, banana, honey, cayenne, ginger, and salt in a blender until smooth. Add water 1 tablespoon (15 milliliters) at a time to adjust the consistency to taste. Serve immediately.

Note: The hemp seeds may be replaced by raw almonds, raw cashews, or raw sunflower seeds. Soak the nuts or seeds in water for about 10 minutes or until softened prior to proceeding with the recipe.

Serves 2

YOUNG MEE RIM & RASMUS LAURVIG

{ STUDENTS }

Young Mee Rim and Rasmus Laurvig live in a brimming apartment. The walls are lined with vintage wallpaper and rows of stacked books. Antlers and taxidermied small animals fill the gaps between the books, the records, and the vintage cameras. Black-and-white photos on the shelves pay homage to old family memories. Their place is small, but it is filled with evidence of lives well lived: stories read, records spun, photographs snapped. Young and Rasmus's apartment is alive with their love and their loves. Entering this place is an intimate invitation into their shared life.

They have a kitchen, a bedroom, a bathroom, and a dining room. There is no big-screen television, no plush sofa. There is, however, a table perfectly decorated, with chairs enough for a few friends and room enough for a meal. Their dining room is where they do their living—around the table and over food, reminding us that the dining room, in fact, is the truest form of a living room. It's where we grow, are nourished, and connect with one another.

The pair makes us a special Danish cookie, with layers of buttery sweetness, jam, and meringue. We discuss the merits of Bob Dylan and Patti Smith over tiny cups of coffee. We share an ordinary conversation—that feels meaningful—with new friends we didn't know only one hour earlier. With this couple, you come for an hour and stay all night.

I heard they used to host weekly Uno nights, a ritual anyone can engage in, anywhere. As we discovered with Young and Rasmus, and they probably discovered with their weekly card games, hospitality transcends borders. Open your doors, make your home inviting, and relationships will grow. •

Meringue-Raspberry Bars

9 tablespoons (4½ ounces/ 125 grams) salted butter, at room temperature

1 cup plus 3 tablespoons (8½ ounces/240 grams) sugar

2 large eggs, separated and at room temperature

1½ cups (7½ ounces/210 grams) all-purpose flour

Raspberry jam or compote

Position a rack in the center of the oven and preheat the oven to 350°F (177°C).

Mix the butter, half of the sugar, the egg yolks, and the flour until they form a dough. Roll it out directly onto a small baking sheet (about 12 by 6 inches/30 by 15 centimeters). Alternatively, break the dough into small pieces, scatter them on the sheet, press them down into an even layer, and then use the back of a spoon to smooth it out.

Bake the dough for 5 minutes or until just beginning to crisp. Transfer the sheet to a rack. Reduce the oven temperature to 300°F (150°C).

Beat the egg whites with an electric mixer fitted with the whisk attachment on medium speed for 1 minute or until they begin to foam. With the mixer running, add the remaining sugar in a slow, steady stream and continue beating for 2 to 3 minutes or until the egg whites are glossy and hold stiff peaks.

Spread raspberry jam to taste over the cookie base, then gently spread the meringue on top of the jam. Bake for about 1 hour or until the meringue is dry and lightly golden. Transfer to a rack and cool completely, at least 1 hour. Cut the cookies into 12 to 16 bars or rounds and serve.

Makes 12 to 16 bars

IDA & LASSE LÆRKE

{ PHOTOGRAPHER AND STUDENT }

With hundreds of thousands of followers on Instagram, Ida Lærke has become an international icon for phone photography. People across the globe tune in to view her still lifes, her clothes, her walks through natural landscapes. Amazingly, Ida is not a trained photographer. She does not own a camera other than the one on her phone, and she has never studied ISO or aperture. The platform of social media has given us the opportunity to appreciate her natural aesthetic vision and skill from our own living rooms.

We met Ida at her apartment, where she welcomed us with Saxo, her young son, clinging to her leg. Within an instant, Saxo was chasing us around the apartment, showing us his recent drawings, and climbing on his bunk bed. Ida's husband, Lasse, made coffee as we settled into a morning of easy conversation and laughter. Both Ida and Lasse are students with passions outside their university studies, Ida's in Instagram photography and Lasse's in cycling—whether it be collecting and refurbishing bikes or leading his young family around Copenhagen and throughout the country on bicycle outings.

This family is tightly knit—Ida and Lasse sip coffee together every morning, and they make meals as a team, with Saxo even helping out occasionally. Among their friends they were pioneers on the parenthood front, which led them to invite friends over more often instead of getting together at a restaurant or bar. They joke about how many bottles of red wine have been consumed around their table with those friends while little Saxo sleeps peacefully in the other room. This bright and airy apartment is the stage on which they have created a community. ◆

Smørrebrød
(Open-Faced Sandwich)

FOR THE MAYONNAISE

1 large egg yolk, at room temperature

1 teaspoon (5 grams) Dijon mustard

1 to 2 teaspoons (5 to 10 milliliters) vinegar

1 teaspoon (5 milliliters) fresh lemon juice

1 cup plus 2 tablespoons (300 milliliters) vegetable oil

Salt and freshly ground black pepper

FOR THE SANDWICH

1 slice rye bread

1 leafy green lettuce leaf

½ hard-boiled egg

¼ cup (about 1 ounce/30 grams) small cooked shrimp, chilled

¼ cup (about 1½ ounces/ 45 grams) grape or cherry tomatoes, halved

A few slices of red onion

Salt and freshly ground black pepper

IDA: *Denmark is famous for its open-faced sandwiches made on rye bread. We eat them for breakfast as well as lunch almost every day. They can be varied infinitely, but a slice of rye bread is always the foundation of the sandwiches we make.*

This recipe is for a lettuce, shrimp, tomato, and mayonnaise sandwich, and the amounts of ingredients and toppings can be adjusted to taste. These are a few pairing suggestions you might also like to try: smoked salmon with cream cheese and cress; sliced boiled new potatoes with mayonnaise and chives; and Danish meatballs (frikadeller) *with pickled beets.*

FOR THE MAYONNAISE

Wrap a damp towel around the base of a medium bowl to keep it steady. Whisk together the egg yolk, mustard, vinegar, and lemon juice. Add the oil in a slow, steady stream, whisking constantly. Season with salt and pepper to taste. Refrigerate in a sealed container for up to 2 days.

FOR THE SANDWICH

Place the lettuce on the bread slice. Top with the egg, shrimp, tomatoes, and onion and season with salt and pepper to taste. Dollop with mayonnaise to taste. Serve immediately.

Makes 1 open-faced sandwich

Buttermilk with Sweet Biscuits

FOR THE BISCUITS

2 cups plus 2 tablespoons
(10.6 ounces/300 grams) all-
purpose flour, plus additional
for dusting

½ cup (3½ ounces/100 grams)
sugar

2 teaspoons (6 grams) baking
powder

½ vanilla bean, split lengthwise
and seeds scraped

7 tablespoons (3½ ounces/
100 grams) unsalted butter,
cut into 8 pieces and at room
temperature

1 large egg

3 tablespoons (45 milliliters)
whole milk

FOR THE BUTTERMILK

6 large egg yolks

½ cup (3½ ounces/100 grams)
sugar

1 vanilla bean, split lengthwise
and seeds scraped

Salt

2 cups plus 1 tablespoon
(500 milliliters) buttermilk

2 cups plus 1 tablespoon
(16½ ounces/470 grams) full-fat
yogurt

Grated zest and juice of 1 lemon

IDA: *This is a traditional Danish summer dish, which, as far as we know, is not found anywhere else in the world. There are many variations, but we consider this one with lemon the best served first thing in the morning for breakfast.*

FOR THE BISCUITS

Position a rack in the center of the oven and preheat the oven to 350°F (170°C). Line a baking sheet with parchment paper.

Whisk the flour, sugar, baking powder, and vanilla seeds together in a large bowl. Add the butter and stir until the mixture comes together. Whisk the egg and milk together in a small bowl, then stir the mixture into the dough. Lightly dust a clean, dry work surface with flour. Turn the dough out and knead it just until combined. With a floured rolling pin, roll it out into a circle ⅜ inch (1 centimeter) thick. Flour a ¾-inch (2-centimeter) round cookie cutter, stamp out the biscuits, and arrange them about 1 inch (2.5 centimeters) apart on the prepared sheet.

Bake for 10 minutes, then transfer the baking sheet to a rack and cut them in half lengthwise. Decrease the oven temperature to 212°F (100°C) and return the biscuits to the oven for about 45 minutes or until crisp and completely dry. Transfer to a rack and cool completely, about 30 minutes.

FOR THE BUTTERMILK AND SERVING

Whisk the egg yolks, sugar, vanilla seeds, and a pinch of salt in a medium bowl until the mixture becomes thick and pale yellow.

Whisk the buttermilk and yogurt together in a large bowl. Whisk in about three-quarters of the egg mixture and three-quarters of the lemon zest and juice. Stir in more of the egg mixture and lemon zest and juice to adjust the consistency and flavor to taste.

Cover the bowl with plastic wrap and refrigerate for about 2 hours or until completely chilled.

Serve the buttermilk with the sweet biscuits on top.

Serves 4 to 6

EBBE JØRGENSEN

{ RETIRED BUSINESSMAN }

Miles and miles outside of Copenhagen, down gravel roads and past a small pastoral village, Ebbe Jørgensen's property sits between farmlands and pastures. His sprawling acreage is home to horses, a dog named Othello, many frequently visiting grandchildren, and of course, Ebbe himself. His home is just one part of the whole here; the residence is squared off by three large barns, creating a courtyard just outside his front door. In this courtyard, Othello presides under a blooming apple tree.

In one barn, Ebbe has built a swimming pool. In another, a party hall. The vision for this land, spawned by Ebbe and his late wife, was to create not a utopia—although it may feel like one—but a place where their children would want to come, even as adults. Their grandchildren, too. And come they have, for every holiday and special occasion as well as casual family meals. They come from all corners of the world for vegetable picking, horseback riding, and the bucolic beauty.

Ebbe has the life that many of us covet. His world is the product of a lifetime spent in simple hospitality, closeness to the earth, and hard work—of both the mind and the body. He told us almost prophetically that if you care to learn from his land, you will learn much. And we did by plucking tomatoes from the vine, chopping beets, gathering greenery and flowers for wild bouquet centerpieces. We learned that hospitality means investing in one another, that food need not be complicated to be good, and that horses grazing in rolling grasslands make the perfect backdrop for a summer lunch. If we are attentive to what nature, food, friends, and family have to teach us, there is much to be learned, particularly from individuals like Ebbe. ◆

CPNHGN

Ebbe's Summer Menu

Danish Open-Faced Sandwiches: A loaf of freshly baked Danish rye bread—dark, fragrant, and flecked with fleshy caraway seeds—lays the foundation for Ebbe's sandwiches. Thin slices of the hearty, textured bread are then layered with an array of toppings and served open-faced. Two of Ebbe's favorite combinations are sliced potato, mayonnaise, and chives and crimson beets, mayonnaise, and fresh thyme. All ingredients are farm-to-table at their most honest, with vegetables and herbs taken directly from the earth on Ebbe's farm.

Mackerel in Tomato Sauce: The heart of this recipe lies in the sourcing of the freshest of ingredients, namely fish and vegetables. Prepare the mackerel as desired, then prepare a simple sauce of sliced tomatoes and yellow onions, sautéed in olive oil until soft and melting. Portion the fish and top it with the sauce, passing lemon wedges and coarse salt at the table. A simple salad of market greens and herbs like lovage and parsley is the only accompaniment this meal needs.

MORTEN SVENDSEN

{ CO-OWNER, WERKSTETTE }

The rumor around town goes that if Morten Svendsen invites you to dinner, you go to dinner. Regardless of prior commitments or conflicts, you attend because you know you will not be disappointed. The kitchen itself is something to behold. As he reconceptualized the layout of his Danish apartment, Morten knocked down walls, moved a bathroom, added infinitely more counter space, and created what might be considered the greatest private kitchen in all of Copenhagen. Grand high ceilings give way to hanging pots and pans, as counters, stoves, and sinks wrap around the walls of the room. Our eyes are drawn both upward and outward. Amid a wealth of ironclad beauty, the kitchen spills into a dining area at the center of which is a long table. Morten saw the potential of his traditional and boxy city apartment and overhauled the place to fit the life of hosting, cooking, and dining communally. He is a visionary, an observer, and a progressive thinker, ready to challenge expectations of how a kitchen should be constructed or what role the dining room should play in a home.

There is ample room at the counter for all the guests to help chop, prepare, ladle, serve. We all gather around to contribute, standing next to others we've just met. Helpers stand over the butcher block, over the sink, over the stove. Morten himself floats from station to station, quietly observing and leading the meal preparation. He has an experience in mind, and it's one that he is curating as he goes. This is an experience that includes the prepping of the food, a long dinner composed of many courses, and postprandial rounds of flaming sambuca and French-pressed coffee. All the while, the tall tapered candles are burning now down at their base, wax cascading onto the table. We stay here until the night moves into its darkest hour. We linger, not wanting to leave. It is apparent in every corner of his home and in every dish or drink that is served that dining with Morten is an experience unto itself. If we are ever fortunate enough to be invited again, regardless of prior commitments or conflicts, we will go. ◆

Beef Brisket Broth with Meatballs and Dumplings

Dumpling recipe adapted from the cookbook *God Mad Let at Lave (Good Food, Easy to Do)*

FOR THE BROTH

6.6 pounds (3 kilograms) boneless beef brisket

2 medium yellow onions, peeled and cut in half

2 teaspoons (0.09 ounce/ 2.6 grams) black peppercorns

1 teaspoon (0.04 ounce/1 gram) coriander seeds

6 parsley stems

1 small bunch of fresh thyme

Leafy tops of 1 celery root, washed

2 bay leaves

Salt and freshly ground black pepper

FOR THE VEGETABLES

8 ounces (230 grams) carrots, diced

1 celery root, peeled and cut into small dice

3 large leeks, white parts only, coarsely chopped

MORTEN: *This broth as a traditional meal comes with leeks, carrots, celeriac (celery root), meatballs, and dumplings. You can add your favorite vegetables as you like, and it is best served with bread.*

FOR THE BROTH

Place the brisket in a large pot. Add enough cold water to cover the brisket by 2 inches (5 centimeters). Add the onion halves, peppercorns, and coriander seeds. Tie the parsley stems, thyme, celery root top, and bay leaves together with kitchen twine and add to the pot. Bring the mixture to a boil and immediately reduce the heat to medium-low.

Simmer the brisket, skimming the surface occasionally, for 4 hours or until tender.

Transfer the beef to a cutting board to cool, then wrap in plastic wrap, refrigerate, and reserve for another use. Strain the broth into a bowl and return it to the pot, reserving 3½ ounces (100 milliliters) for the dumplings. Season the broth with salt and pepper to taste.

Add the vegetables to the broth and cook over medium heat for 15 minutes or until tender.

FOR THE MEATBALLS

Combine the pork, veal, eggs, flour, salt, and pepper in a medium bowl. Shape ¾-inch (2-centimeter) balls of the mixture and drop gently into the simmering broth. Simmer until cooked through, about 5 minutes.

FOR THE MEATBALLS

1½ pounds (680 grams) finely minced or ground pork

1½ pounds (680 grams) finely minced or ground veal

2 large eggs, beaten

2 tablespoons (0.6 ounce/ 18 grams) all-purpose flour

1 teaspoon (6 grams) salt

¼ teaspoon freshly ground black pepper

FOR THE DUMPLINGS

1½ teaspoons (9 grams) salt

2 tablespoons (1 ounce/ 30 grams) unsalted butter, melted

3½ ounces (100 milliliters) beef broth (from recipe here)

3 large eggs

6 tablespoons (2 ounces/ 60 grams) all-purpose flour

FOR THE DUMPLINGS

Bring 4 quarts (4 liters) water and 1 teaspoon (6 grams) of the salt to a boil in a large pot. Reduce the heat to medium-low to keep the water simmering. Prepare an ice bath by combining equal amounts of cold water and ice cubes in a large bowl.

Whisk the butter, the 3½ ounces reserved broth, the eggs, and the remaining ½ teaspoon (3 grams) salt in a small bowl. Place the flour in a medium bowl and whisk in the liquid mixture; mix just until combined.

Using a 1-teaspoon (5-milliliter) measure, spoon dumplings into the simmering water and cook until they rise to the surface, about 3 minutes. Transfer the dumplings to the ice bath and allow to cool completely, then transfer to a paper-towel-lined plate with a slotted spoon.

TO SERVE

Ladle broth and vegetables into bowls. Add the dumplings and warm through, about 3 minutes. Serve.

Pictured on page 150
Serves 10

TURE ANDERSEN

{ PHOTOGRAPHER }

Ture Andersen has made his home on the water. Much of his year is spent kayaking and photographing around Greenland, but when he is home, he resides in a houseboat hidden along the canals of Copenhagen. The houseboat, a refurbished ferry that operated in the middle of the century, provides shelter and adventure for Ture and his two young sons, Robert and Karl. The boys alternate between snagging crabs in nets and casting lines off the side of the boat—apparently they, too, connect with water. This combined home and boat has been completely overhauled, making room for a breezy kitchen, an open dining area, rustic wood floors, and cozy reading nooks. The glass-paned ceiling allows the waning summer sun to fill the home.

The dinner table is set on the open-ended bow. We take turns rocking in the hammock and scouting for fish with the boys. Dinner is simple and inspired by Ture's lifestyle. The food is picked from his own garden and caught in the water out his front door. And Ture lets that food speak for itself. "If you have good ingredients," he says, "you keep it simple." His salad was comprised of fresh lettuce drizzled with truffle oil and olive oil and sprinkled with olives, slices of Parmesan, and salt and pepper. His fish and meats were prepared in an oil-and-herb marinade and then grilled over an open flame. Nothing too glamorous or unavailable; he simply lets the food speak for itself.

We picked through every morsel left on the table as the sun disappeared below the horizon, taking with it the warmth. We bundled up in blankets and sweaters to continue our outdoor visit. Ture regaled us with stories, among them about his snapping a surreptitious photograph of Castro and kayaking around Greenland with his son in his lap. We were a captive audience, clutching our little glasses of white wine, huddled over the table. This is how Ture lives, and it's the place where a man of adventure shapes a dwelling of adventure. His life on the houseboat is a comfortable yet offbeat existence—in tune with the natural rhythms of the earth, the tides, and the soil. ◆

Ture's Summer Menu for the Ferry

Summer, the salt air, the melting orange afternoon sun, and a ferry ride. The scene is set and appetites are sharpened by the wind and brine. Ture Andersen relies on fresh and local ingredients to feed family and friends.

Even when he was a child, food captured Ture's attention. As an adult with schedules and time constraints, he still carves out moments to really relish meals, beginning with the search for produce that is organic and local.

He and his family have a varied diet that includes vegetarian and meat-based options. In addition, they eat fish twice a week: he catches cod and mackerel directly from the ferry and quickly tosses a light salad with fresh greens and fruit for the side. Always, the meal is accompanied by the family's rye bread, made with a thirty-year-old sourdough starter and 100 percent rye flour.

Fish: Place a side of your favorite fish—Ture recommends organic Scottish salmon for its flavor and fine, velvety texture—in a casserole dish and drizzle it with olive oil, white wine, salt, pepper, and fresh herbs. Cover the casserole with foil and bake the fish at 392°F (200°C) for 20 minutes, until opaque and firm on the outside and fleshy and translucent in the center. Serve the fish with small new potatoes boiled in heavily salted water and tossed with chopped fresh lovage or flat-leaf parsley.

Lamb Chops: Season organic lamb chops with rosemary, sea salt, and pepper. Drizzle them with olive oil and cook them on a hot grill for 1 to 2 minutes per side or until they are cooked to desired doneness.

Arrange the chops on a platter and serve them with thinly sliced zucchini sprinkled with chopped rosemary or small new potatoes boiled in heavily salted water and tossed with chopped fresh lovage or flat-leaf parsley.

Simple Salad with Fennel: Toss organic greens with thinly shaved fennel, sliced pear, salt, pepper, olive and truffle oils, and white balsamic vinegar. Finish the salad with torn basil leaves and shavings of Spanish manchego cheese. Serve with homemade bread.

STEVE MOMSEN

{ CHEF }

Steve Momsen has three important jobs: father, husband, and cook. An accomplished self-employed chef, Steve works at a local business during the week, providing innovative and fresh lunches for employees. This schedule means he's home on the weekends and, just as important, home for dinner with his wife, Anna, and their two small children, Markus and Leah.

We arrived at Steve and Anna's house on a cool September evening and were greeted by the precocious Markus babbling Danish pleasantries. We lingered in the kitchen, wandered through the garden, and snacked on Danish sweet peas as Steve prepared the meal. More friends arrived, and eventually casual small talk turned into genuine conversations. The evening progressed, and over many courses our new acquaintances became our new friends.

"I don't really use recipes, only when baking. I try to encourage others to think outside of recipes and get comfortable with making their own, or changing existing ones." —STEVE MOMSEN

Steve's food warmed our bodies, and the savory aromas filled the kitchen and dining room. His food was unique, blending flavors from China to India, America to Denmark. He himself is Australian, while his wife is Danish. It seems that his food, as well as his melded family, reflects this beautiful cultural union.

After second helpings were finished and the last bowl was licked, we retired to the living room, where tapered candles, bottles of fine port, and sweet Danish treats awaited us. The hours passed even more quickly here in a blur of engaging conversation, uproarious laughter, and cigar smoke. The hospitality of Steve and Anna is founded on the belief that nourishing food and meaningful conversation keep a person engaged, full, and at home.

We came out of our cozy trance at midnight; back to reality, back to train schedules. We ran to catch the 12:30 train to the city center, wishing we could linger in the Momsen living room all night, and move directly into heaps of eggs and ham in the morning. Anna and Steve's easy hospitality meant we arrived as strangers and departed as a part of their community. ◆

"When I first came to Denmark, in 2004, I worked for a chef called Erwin Lauterbach. He taught me how to taste. It's important that a meal include the five tastes: salt, sweet, bitter, sour, and umami. For example, if you are making a creamy pumpkin soup, a squeeze of lemon juice at the end will bring your soup to another level. You don't want it to taste sour, but the acid of the lemon acts as a flavor enhancer, just as you use salt to enhance flavor. I believe this to be an important lesson of cooking, to learn what different ingredients taste of and thereby be able to create new dishes without recipes."

—STEVE MOMSEN

Grilled Salmon with Romesco Sauce and Fennel Crudités

FOR THE SAUCE

4 red bell peppers, ribs and seeds removed, cut into chunks

2 vine-ripened tomatoes, cut into wedges

5 tablespoons (75 milliliters) extra-virgin olive oil

Salt and freshly ground black pepper

1 cup (6 ounces/170 grams) whole roasted almonds

2 tablespoons (30 milliliters) sherry vinegar or balsamic vinegar

1 garlic clove, peeled and smashed

1 tablespoon (0.1 ounce/ 3 grams) chopped fresh herbs, such as dill, parsley, chives, or chervil

STEVE: *This combination is a hit. The Spanish romesco sauce is also good as a dip, in a sandwich, tossed in pasta, or with just about anything. The fennel and apple crudités gives the dish texture and freshness.*

FOR THE SAUCE

Position a rack in the center of the oven and preheat the oven to 480°F (249°C).

Toss the peppers and tomatoes with 3 tablespoons (45 milliliters) of the olive oil on a foil-lined baking sheet; season the mixture with salt and pepper.

Roast for 10 to 15 minutes, stirring the mixture halfway through the roasting time, or until the peppers are well browned and the tomatoes are soft. Transfer the sheet to a rack and cool for 15 minutes.

Pulse the pepper-tomato mixture, almonds, vinegar, garlic, herbs, and remaining 2 tablespoons (30 milliliters) olive oil in a food processor until a thick paste is formed. Season with salt and pepper. The romesco can be made up to 2 days in advance and refrigerated in an airtight container.

FOR THE SALMON

2 pounds (910 grams) skin-on salmon, cut into 6 fillets

2 tablespoons (30 milliliters) vegetable oil

Salt and freshly ground black pepper

FOR THE CRUDITÉS

1 fennel bulb

1 apple, peeled, cored, and cut into matchsticks

¼ cup (0.4 ounce/10 grams) fresh dill, chopped

Juice of 1 lemon

Salt and freshly ground black pepper

FOR THE SALMON

Light a charcoal grill and allow the coals to turn ashy and white. If using a gas grill, heat it to medium-high according to the manufacturer's instructions. Brush the salmon fillets with the vegetable oil and season with salt and pepper.

Cook the salmon for 2 to 3 minutes on each side or until it has grill marks and the flesh begins to turn opaque. Carefully transfer the fillets to a serving platter with a thin metal spatula. Cover loosely with foil.

FOR THE CRUDITÉS AND SERVING

Cut off and discard the fennel stalk, cut out the tough core, and slice the bulb ⅛ inch (0.37 centimeter) thick, preferably on a mandoline. Toss the fennel, apple, dill, and lemon juice together in a medium bowl. Season with salt and pepper to taste.

Spread a generous spoonful of the romesco on each of 6 plates, then top with salmon. Serve the crudités alongside.

Pictured on page 163
Serves 6

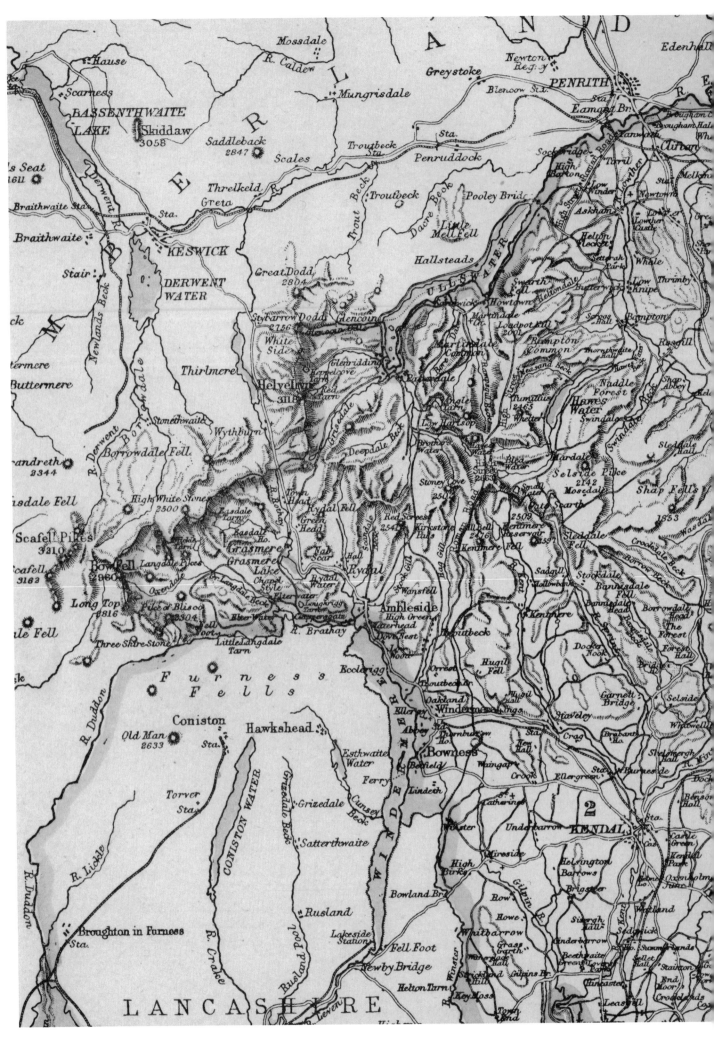

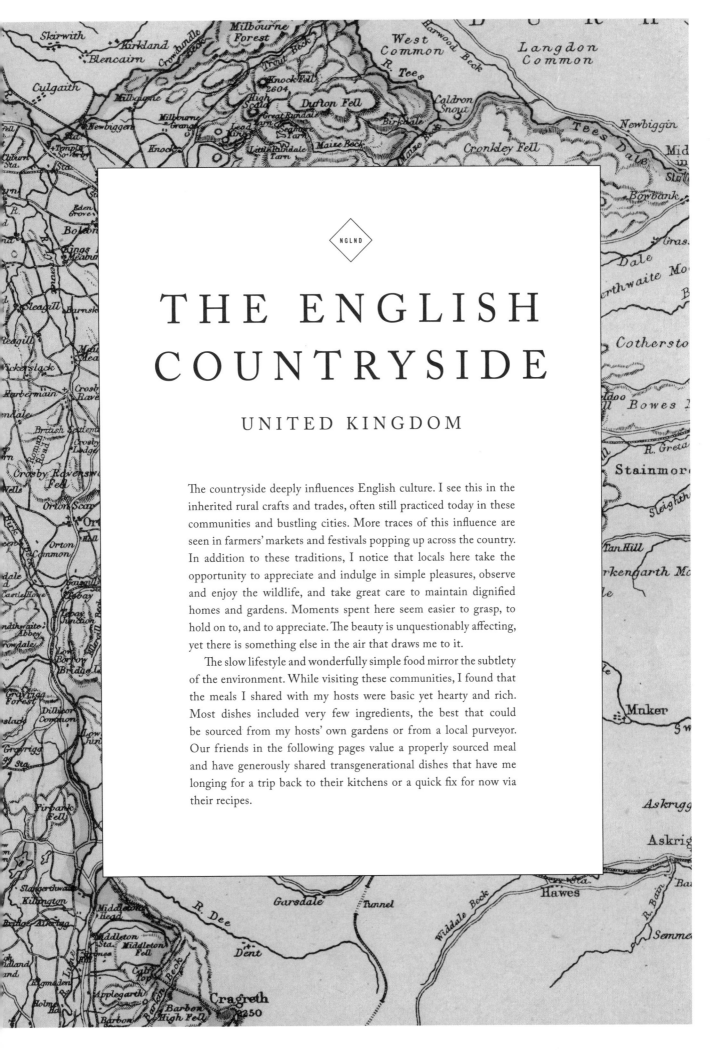

NGLND

THE ENGLISH COUNTRYSIDE

UNITED KINGDOM

The countryside deeply influences English culture. I see this in the inherited rural crafts and trades, often still practiced today in these communities and bustling cities. More traces of this influence are seen in farmers' markets and festivals popping up across the country. In addition to these traditions, I notice that locals here take the opportunity to appreciate and indulge in simple pleasures, observe and enjoy the wildlife, and take great care to maintain dignified homes and gardens. Moments spent here seem easier to grasp, to hold on to, and to appreciate. The beauty is unquestionably affecting, yet there is something else in the air that draws me to it.

The slow lifestyle and wonderfully simple food mirror the subtlety of the environment. While visiting these communities, I found that the meals I shared with my hosts were basic yet hearty and rich. Most dishes included very few ingredients, the best that could be sourced from my hosts' own gardens or from a local purveyor. Our friends in the following pages value a properly sourced meal and have generously shared transgenerational dishes that have me longing for a trip back to their kitchens or a quick fix for now via their recipes.

SAM WYLDE

{ RESTAURATEUR }

Every town should have a resource like Sam's Kitchen. A meeting place in Bath with constantly evolving menus, Sam's Kitchen is a go-to spot for locally sourced food and artisanal treats. The restaurant is intimate and homey, open during the week for lunch and on Friday nights for live music and tapas. There are no individual tables, just a family-style communal one, and once the food is gone, it's gone. The space has played host to pop-up restaurants and supper clubs and is also available to rent out for catered parties and other gatherings.

Sam Wylde, proprietor and founder of his namesake restaurant, is laid back and approachable. He lives with his young daughter, Florence, in a historic town house in Bath, and constantly brings home delicacies and innovative new recipes to sample. Sam is moving forward in his culinary art, excelling in his craft of cooking and taking local residents along with him.

He has owned farmland with his family for more than fifteen years, and that farm supplies a significant amount of the restaurant's produce. Over the past several years, however, the farm has also started raising pigs, whose meat is used in the restaurant and sold at farmers' markets around the region. The land holds higher aims still, as Sam has begun to plan special events there, beginning with a Pig Feast paired with local wines and farm-pressed cider.

Sam's Kitchen represents more of a movement than a mere restaurant. It distinguishes itself not only in the freshness of the food but also in the finely tuned rhythm of cooking with the seasons. This commitment ensures that Sam's food is richly flavorful but not complicated, wholesome and natural though not contrived. Whether in the city or on the farm, Sam and his kitchen are worth a visit. ◦

Pot Roast Shoulder of Veal with Tuna Sauce

FOR THE VEAL

2 tablespoons (30 milliliters) olive oil

4⅓ pounds (2 kilograms) boned, rolled, and tied veal shoulder roast

Salt and freshly ground black pepper

1 large white onion, peeled and cut into 6 wedges

1 large carrot, peeled and cut into 2-inch (5-centimeter) pieces

1 celery stalk, cut into 2-inch (5-centimeter) pieces

¾ cup (180 milliliters) dry white wine

1 bay leaf

FOR THE SAUCE

Two 5-ounce (140-gram) cans high-quality oil-packed tuna, drained

Yolks from 2 hard-boiled large eggs

2 salt-packed anchovy fillets, rinsed and patted dry

10 fresh tarragon leaves

4 fresh basil leaves

4 fresh mint leaves

1 tablespoon (15 milliliters) tarragon or white wine vinegar

1 tablespoon (15 milliliters) olive oil

Juice of ½ lemon

1 tablespoon plus 1 teaspoon (0.7 ounce/20 grams) salt-packed capers, rinsed and patted dry

Salt and freshly ground black pepper

FOR THE VEAL

Position a rack in the center of the oven and preheat the oven to 338°F (170°C).

Heat the olive oil in a large, heavy pot or Dutch oven over medium-high heat until beginning to smoke. Season the veal with salt and pepper and cook it for 12 to 15 minutes or until well browned on all sides, then transfer it to a plate. Add the onion, carrot, and celery to the pot and cook, stirring, for 5 minutes or until browned.

Add the wine, scrape the bottom of the pan to release any browned bits, then simmer until reduced by half. Return the veal and any accumulated juices to the pot. Add the bay leaf and enough water to cover the veal by 1 inch (2.5 centimeters). Bring the mixture to a boil, then cover the pot and place it in the oven for 2½ hours or until the veal is tender. Transfer it to a platter and allow it to rest for 20 minutes.

FOR THE SAUCE AND SERVING

While the veal rests, strain the cooking liquid into a bowl and discard the solids. Process the tuna, egg yolks, anchovies, tarragon, basil, mint, vinegar, olive oil, and lemon juice, and half of the capers in a food processor until smooth. Add 1 cup (240 milliliters) of the veal-cooking liquid and pulse to combine. Stir in additional cooking liquid to adjust the sauce's consistency to taste (it should be pourable but thick). Stir in the remaining half of the capers and season to taste with salt and pepper.

Thinly slice the veal and serve with the tuna sauce.

Pictured on page 170
Serves 4 to 6

Roasted Butternut Squash, Urfa Chile, and Buffalo Mozzarella Salad

1 large butternut squash, scrubbed and seeded

3 tablespoons (45 milliliters) rapeseed oil, plus additional for finishing

2 garlic cloves, peeled and smashed

2 teaspoons (5 grams) Urfa chile flakes

2 fresh thyme sprigs

Sea salt and freshly ground black pepper

One 8-ounce (230-gram) ball buffalo mozzarella

4 cups (4 ounces/115 grams) arugula or baby spinach leaves

SAM: *This is a warming, hearty, and simple salad that is great as a side or perfect piled on a plate. The Urfa chiles add a great smoky, tobaccolike flavor but don't have blow-your-head-off heat!*

Position a rack in the center of the oven and preheat the oven to 325°F (218°C). Line a 13-by-9-inch (33-by-23-centimeter) baking pan with parchment paper.

Cut the squash crosswise into slices 2 inches (5 centimeters) thick. Toss the slices in a large bowl with the 3 tablespoons rapeseed oil, the garlic, Urfa chile, and thyme. Season with salt and pepper and arrange in the prepared pan, skin side down.

Bake for 20 to 25 minutes or until the squash is caramelized on the edges and tender but firm. Transfer the pan to a rack and cool for 5 minutes.

Pull the mozzarella ball apart and toss it on top of the squash along with the arugula. Drizzle with more rapeseed oil if desired and toss lightly to combine everything. Season with salt and pepper to taste and serve.

Serves 4 as an appetizer or side dish

SILVANA DE SOISSONS

{ FOUNDING EDITOR, *THE FOODIE BUGLE* }

You'll find Silvana de Soissons where English sensibilities meet Italian passion. The bubbling and exuberant editor of Britain's popular online magazine *The Foodie Bugle*, Silvana is infectious. She greets you with her little dogs by her side and with hugs and pints of local ales. Her home, named Bicknoll House—located in Wiltshire, in the provincial countryside of southeastern England—was originally constructed in the middle of the eighteenth century. Staying true to the history of the home and to her geography at large, she has created a countryside paradise, outfitted with a host of wellies for visitors and jelly molds by the dozens.

Every room, corner, and wall has Silvana written on it. Decoupaged bathrooms, stacks of striped tea towels, teakettles in various blues and yellows—all reflect her pastoral and eclectic style. This is a woman who has mastered the art of making a house a home, not only for herself, her husband, and her daughter, but also for all weary travelers and transient visitors.

In her role as editor and founder of *The Foodie Bugle*, Silvana often finds herself hosting lunches, teas, and casual get-togethers with other food-minded individuals. She created the magazine in an effort to "tell the whole story of simple, frugal, seasonal food and drink from farm to fork." She provides an accessible resource with quality writing, which spotlights freshly grown produce around the country and the artisans who use these ingredients to make their own offerings. Her leadership and vision established *The Foodie Bugle* as a pioneer in England's food culture; it won the Guild of Food Writers New Media Award in 2012.

Though we stayed with her for only a few days, we could have stayed through the winter, huddled over books in the drawing room, warming our stocking feet by the fire. Silvana's world is charming and bucolic, nourished by good food and brought to life by her own spurts of laughter. Leaving here was not unlike leaving home—in the hope and expectation that you will, one day, return. ◆

Almond and Pistachio Biscuits

10 tablespoons (5 ounces/
140 grams) unsalted butter, at
room temperature

½ cup (3½ ounces/100 grams)
superfine sugar

1½ cups (7½ ounces/210 grams)
all-purpose flour, sifted, plus
additional for dusting

½ cup (2 ounces/60 grams)
shelled raw pistachios, finely
ground

⅓ cup (2 ounces/60 grams)
blanched almonds, finely ground

1 vanilla bean, slit lengthwise,
seeds scraped out

Grated zest of 1 lemon

Confectioners' sugar, for dusting

Position a rack in the center of the oven and preheat the oven to 350°F (177°C). Line two baking sheets with parchment paper and brush with 2 tablespoons (28 grams) of the butter.

Beat the remaining 8 tablespoons (1 stick/112 grams) butter and the sugar with an electric mixer on medium speed until light and fluffy, about 3 minutes. Pause the mixer and add the flour, nuts, vanilla bean seeds, and lemon zest. Beat on low speed just until the ingredients come together, then gather the dough and knead just to form a cohesive dough.

Lightly coat your hands with flour and divide the dough into 24 pieces. Roll each piece into a ball between your palms, flouring them as needed. Arrange 12 balls on each of the prepared baking sheets, spacing them about 1 inch (2.5 centimeters) apart.

Bake the biscuits for about 15 minutes or until pale golden. Transfer the sheets to racks and cool on the sheets for about 15 minutes. Sift confectioners' sugar over the biscuits and serve.

Makes 24 biscuits

ROSA PARK

{ FOOD WRITER }

Bath might be the most charming town not just in England but in the world. With its uniform stone buildings and Georgian architecture, it's as historic as it is aesthetic. Situated in the middle of town, the Royal Crescent is a stunning arched façade of town houses, offices, and even a hotel. It is here that Rosa Park, a spirited writer and food lover, lives with her boyfriend, food photographer/filmmaker Richard Stapleton. Rosa runs an impressive travel and food magazine called *Cereal*, which entails chasing down restaurateurs, styling perfect autumnal picnics, and tasting all the tea England offers.

Being born in Seoul, South Korea, growing up in Vancouver, Canada, and traveling throughout her life has made Rosa as cultured as she is inclusive and outgoing. She leads conversations with a writerly intent—to dig deep, to ask provocative questions, and to stimulate healthy and challenging dialogue. Her gifts support her writing and strengthen her relationship with Richard while the two make time in their busy days for fine dining and drinking tea.

Greatly influenced by her father, who she claims is the best cook she has ever known, Rosa believes that making food for yourself is always better than buying it—because even the "bad" foods are not so bad when you put time and love into making them come alive. Rosa makes food come alive, whether while feeding fortunate friends or writing about the restaurants and purveyors that enrich Bath for all. ◆

Steamed Cod

One 6-ounce (170-gram) cod fillet

4 ounces (115 grams) fresh ginger, peeled and cut into matchsticks ⅛ inch (0.3 centimeter) thick

5 scallions, chopped

½ cup (½ ounce/15 grams) fresh cilantro leaves, plus cilantro for garnish

2 teaspoons (10 milliliters) soy sauce

2 teaspoons (10 milliliters) mirin

Freshly ground black pepper

Cut a piece of foil three times the length of the cod. Arrange half of the ginger, half of the scallions, and half of the cilantro on the bottom third of the foil, then set the cod on top.

Place the remaining ginger, scallions, and cilantro on top of the cod, then drizzle with the soy sauce and mirin and season with pepper.

Fold the long part of the foil over the cod and roll the edges to make a sort of envelope. Place the foil packet in a small saucepan and cover. Set the pan over medium heat and cook for 6 to 8 minutes or until the cod is cooked through.

Carefully unwrap the foil packet and transfer the fish and vegetables to a plate. Top with cilantro leaves and serve with steamed rice.

Serves 1

Kimchi Couscous

2 cups (480 milliliters) water

Salt and freshly ground black
pepper

2 teaspoons (10 milliliters) olive
oil

1 cup (6 ounces/170 grams)
couscous

½ cup (about 6 ounces/
170 grams) kimchi, diced

Cilantro leaves

Bring the water to a boil in a small saucepan over medium-high
heat. Add ½ teaspoon (3 grams) salt and 1 teaspoon (5 milliliters) of
the olive oil, stir in the couscous, cover, and remove from the heat.
Allow to rest (covered) for 5 minutes, then fluff with a fork.

Heat the remaining 1 teaspoon (5 milliliters) olive oil in a medium
skillet over medium heat until shimmering. Add the kimchi and
cook, stirring, for about 3 minutes or until the kimchi is heated
through.

Stir the couscous into the kimchi and season with salt and pepper to
taste. Cook, stirring, for 2 to 3 minutes.

Garnish with cilantro leaves and serve hot or at room temperature.

Serves 2

ANNA & TOM HERBERT

{ BAKERY PROPRIETORS }

In the English culinary world, the Herbert family is famous. Owners of Hobbs House Bakery and Butchery in Chipping Sodbury, the Herberts have propagated five generations of masterly bakers, with a sixth generation right on their heels. The patriarch of the family, Trevor Herbert, is a dynamic, engaging man, matched in kind by his gracious wife, Polly. The pair lead their six grown children—including the fabulous baking brothers, Tom and Henry, along with their respective spouses—in a life of discipline, gratitude, baking, and contagious whimsy. The Hobbs House empire has grown exponentially in the past few years. With a TV show, a new cookbook, and a café, the Herbert family is becoming a household name.

Amid this large family, Anna Herbert is quieter than the rest. Wife to Tom, who runs the bakery portion of the business, and the mother to four young, spirited children, Anna juggles much and looks completely at ease doing so. With Tom busy on book tours, judging cooking competitions, or filming for his baking show, she tends to the home and the kids and prepares fresh meals for the family. After challenging herself one year to buy all of their Christmas presents locally, she was converted and now shops locally for all of her family's food.

Anna and Tom's children are skilled yet adventurous; they can bake a loaf of sourdough and then climb a tree in seconds. Their lives are full of joy and adventure. There is something special about this clan, something that radiates from the entire group, particularly when they are all in one room. Their love is effusive, and their connection to one another is palpable. Being in this family's midst meant witnessing a distinct kind of intimacy, so nearly sacred we could not help wanting to be a part of it. ◆

Breakfast Bread

½ cup (120 milliliters) whole milk, warmed to 110° to 115°F (43° to 46°C)

½ cup (4 ounces/120 milliliters) water, warmed to 110° to 115°F (43° to 46°C)

1¼ teaspoons (0.14 ounce/ 4 grams) active dry yeast

3⅓ cups (20 ounces/550 grams) wheat (bread) flour

2 tablespoons (1½ ounces/ 50 grams) honey

2 tablespoons (1 ounce/ 30 grams) butter, at room temperature

Sea salt

1 large egg, at room temperature, plus 1 large egg yolk, for brushing

Line a 9-by-5-inch (23-by-13-centimeter) loaf pan with parchment paper, allowing some excess to hang over the sides.

Stir the milk, water, and yeast together in a small bowl and allow the mixture to stand until it foams, about 10 minutes.

Combine the flour, honey, butter, 2 teaspoons (12 grams) salt, and the whole egg in a large bowl and mix until well combined, then stir in the yeast mixture.

Knead the dough until elastic and slightly sticky, about 15 minutes by hand, 8 minutes with an electric mixer fitted with the dough hook. Return the dough to the bowl, cover it with a dish towel, and allow it to rise in a warm, draft-free place for about 1 hour or until doubled in size.

Shape the dough into an oval, place it in the prepared pan, cover it with plastic wrap, and allow it to rest overnight in the refrigerator.

Position a rack in the center of the oven and preheat the oven to 425°F (218°C). Whisk the egg yolk and brush it over the loaf, then sprinkle with a pinch of sea salt. Place the bread in the oven and generously spray the oven with water (see Note). Bake for 25 to 30 minutes, or until golden. Transfer to a rack and cool for about 15 minutes. Serve warm.

Note: Adding water to the oven creates a steamy environment that allows the bread to bake without the crust's drying out too quickly, producing a taller, fuller loaf. Use a spray bottle to spritz the oven, being mindful to step away to avoid being hit by hot steam.

Makes 1 loaf

Marefield Pie

4 slices (about 3½ ounces/
100 grams) bacon, chopped

4 large ripe tomatoes, peeled
and chopped, or 24 ounces
(680 grams) drained chopped
canned plum tomatoes

2 tablespoons (1 ounce/
30 grams) steel-cut pinhead oats

⅓ cup (0.4 ounce/12 grams)
flat-leaf parsley, chopped (about
3 tablespoons)

Salt and freshly ground black
pepper

TOM: *We highly recommend serving Marefield Pie with either poached
or scrambled eggs, toasted and buttered Breakfast Bread, a dollop of Dijon
mustard, and fresh coffee.*

*This dish is named after a hamlet near Leicester, England. My
grandparents lived there, and my grandfather would often make this
when the family visited. He called all the food he made "pie" and served
a big spoonful of clotted cream on each dish as his signature solution. It
reminds me and my siblings of our grandfather whenever we make it
for breakfast at the start of special days such as weddings and Christmas
morning.*

Cook the bacon in a large skillet over medium-high heat until
beginning to crisp, about 3 minutes. Stir in the tomatoes and
continue to cook, stirring occasionally, until the tomatoes are soft,
about 3 minutes. Stir in the oats, reduce the heat to low, and cook,
stirring occasionally, until they soften, about 10 minutes.

Stir in the parsley and season with salt and pepper to taste. Cover
the skillet, remove it from the heat, and allow the pie to rest for
5 minutes. Serve in shallow bowls.

Notes: Choose bacon that is well streaked with fat.

The mixture should be soft and somewhat loose; add water,
1 tablespoon (15 milliliters) at a time, if at the end of step 1 it
appears too dry.

Serves 2

CARYN HIBBERT

{ RESTAURATEUR }

Caryn Hibbert has a knack for revival. After purchasing an old manor home in Southrop, England, with her husband, she began to buy up the derelict properties surrounding it. One by one, Caryn transformed the forlorn homes, cottages, and stables into an expansive, all-inclusive food lover's paradise. Thyme at Southrop, aptly named for the savory herb, manifests Caryn's passion: a holistic food experience, connected from the soil to the kitchen to the plate. The property's acreage, with her home at the center, features pastures of horses, sheep, and free-range chickens. The grounds include open kitchens, extensive dining tables, cottages, and a manor home for those looking for a longer stay. Guests can take classes to hone their foraging skills or learn to make cheese. The entire estate, while feeling luxurious, is still wild, surrounded by forests, fields, and roaming herds of sheep.

Wife, mother to three nearly grown children, and proprietor of the establishment, Caryn is the perfect combination of purpose and poise. A classic Englishwoman, she is a nurturing mom to her flock of hens and a sharpshooter on the field who commands respect through her countenance and discerning, kind leadership.

Caryn tells us that she used to stress about what to cook when hosting a dinner party, until she realized she didn't need to worry because guests are always so appreciative of having someone cook for them in the first place. This is a bit of sound wisdom we've taken home with us—the virtue of serving others with gratitude and humility instead of insecurity and timidity. ◆

"Sunday lunch is very traditional in our house. All the family will be at home and
help to put together the family feast. We will need to take the dogs on a walk, check
and feed the chickens, collect the eggs, harvest the vegetables, and perhaps pick the
flowers to decorate the table. My favorite Sundays are when we have other families
staying with us so that all generations are together. We will all help and cook
together; it is a lovely, creative, sociable, and relaxing thing to do."

—CARYN HIBBERT

Quick Rosemary Focaccia

2⅓ cups (14 ounces/400 grams) organic strong wheat (bread) flour, plus additional for dusting

1 heaping teaspoon (0.3 ounce/ 8 grams) table salt

2¼ teaspoons (¼ ounce/ 7.5 grams) instant yeast

1¼ cups (300 milliliters) water

⅓ cup plus 1 tablespoon (3.3 ounces/100 milliliters) olive oil

1 small handful of fresh rosemary leaves, coarsely chopped

Maldon salt

Combine the flour, salt, and yeast in a large bowl. Add the water and mix until you have a rough dough. Knead the dough in an electric mixer fitted with the dough hook on medium speed until the dough is elastic and slightly sticky, about 6 minutes. Cover the dough with a dish towel and allow it to rise in a warm, draft-free place for about 1 hour or until doubled in size.

Position a rack in the center of the oven and preheat the oven to 425°F (218°C).

Punch the dough down and cut it in half. Lightly flour a clean, dry work surface and roll the dough out to about 2 inches (5 centimeters) thick. Brush a baking sheet or pizza pan with half of the olive oil. Transfer the dough to the prepared pan and press your fingertips into the dough several times to create indentations on the surface. Brush with the remaining olive oil and sprinkle with the rosemary and Maldon salt. Repeat the procedure with the second piece of dough.

Cover the dough with a dish towel and allow it to rise in a warm, draft-free place for 15 minutes. Bake the bread for 12 to 15 minutes or until golden. Transfer to a rack and cool for 10 minutes. Serve.

Pictured on page 198
Makes 2 focaccia

Rosemary and Anchovy Sauce

Leaves from 1 large bunch of fresh rosemary, finely chopped (about ½ ounce/15 grams)

12 anchovy fillets packed in salt, rinsed and patted dry

2 garlic cloves, peeled

Grated zest and juice of 1 lemon

¾ cup plus 1 tablespoon (200 milliliters) extra-virgin olive oil

CARYN: *This is not a precise recipe; adjust by adding more olive oil or lemon juice to taste. The sauce is delicious with all grilled meats, fish, and vegetables and for dipping bread.*

With a mortar and pestle, crush the rosemary, anchovies, garlic, and lemon zest until a paste forms. (Alternatively, use a food processor to pulse the ingredients together until they form a paste.)

Add the lemon juice and stir until completely incorporated. Slowly add the olive oil and mix vigorously. Serve.

Makes about 1 cup

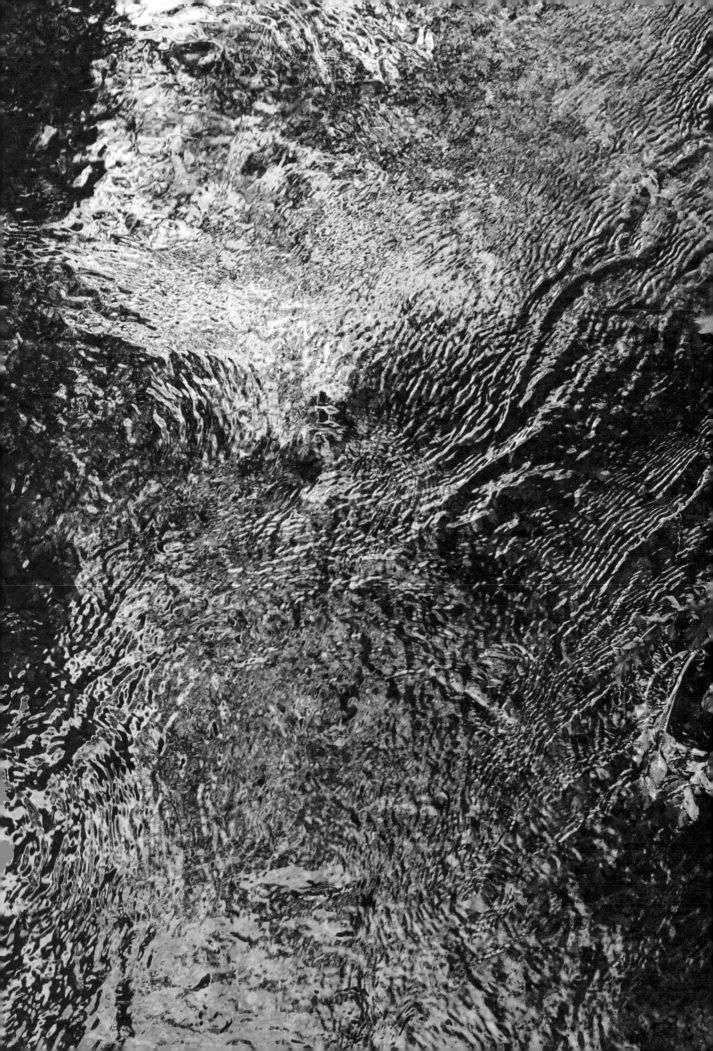

MEL & TOM CALVER

{ SALON OWNER AND CHEESEMAKER }

Mel and Tom Calver are as endearing individually as they are as a couple. Mel owns a salon that has the feel of an artisan boutique, and Tom is a cheesemaker who recently started supplying Jamie Oliver's restaurants with his ricotta. In tandem, this young couple is fiercely creative and intuitively hospitable. They live in a historic town house with five narrow but high-ceilinged floors in Bath. Tom commutes to his family's dairy farm every day, while Mel runs her salon only a few blocks from their charming abode.

The innate disposition Tom and Mel share toward hospitality is seen throughout their home. They have built a wood-fired oven directly into the corner wall of their kitchen, and deep in their cellar they craft hard apple ciders. Their rustic kitchen table accommodates at least a dozen people, which they assure us happens often, as they are both quite sharp in the kitchen. Mel boasts of having been able to cook a roast for an entire dinner party by the age of eight. Tom's expertise as a cheese craftsman has involved years of study and experimentation to perfect each of his flavors.

The two make a mean gin and tonic topped with angostura bitters, as we happily while away a Sunday afternoon with them. Tom cuts us slivers of his various cheeses, and we carve into tender ham hocks. The fire warms the kitchen while Mel and Tom tell us of life in England—the story of how they met when Mel cut Tom's hair and how they were later married wearing wellies. Their life together reflects a partnership that often goes unseen by outsiders—a bond that means they plan Sunday meals together and relish simple pleasures, like sharing coffee and toast topped with portobello mushrooms and Tom's own Caerphilly cheese. Much like the winning food combinations they served us, Mel and Tom are a sweet pair; we came away from our visit with renewed enthusiasm for collaborations of all kinds with those we hold dear. ◆

Lemon Drizzle Cake

FOR THE CAKE

Nonstick baking spray

21 tablespoons (10½ ounces/
300 grams) unsalted butter, at
room temperature

1½ cups (10½ ounces/
300 grams) sugar

Grated zest of 4 lemons

½ teaspoon (5 milliliters) vanilla
extract (or half a vanilla bean
split in half lengthwise, seeds
scraped out)

6 large eggs, at room
temperature

2 cups plus 1 tablespoon
(10½ ounces/300 grams) self-
rising flour

2 tablespoons (30 milliliters)
boiling water

FOR THE GLAZE

1½ cups (10½ ounces/
300 grams) sugar

6 ounces (180 milliliters) fresh
lemon juice

FOR THE CAKE

Position a rack in the center of the oven and preheat the oven to
325°F (163°C). Line a 9-by-5-inch (23-by-13-centimeter) loaf pan
with parchment paper and coat with nonstick baking spray.

Beat the butter, sugar, and lemon zest together in a large bowl with
an electric mixer on medium-high speed for about 3 minutes or until
light and fluffy. Beat in the vanilla extract.

Add the eggs, one at a time, beating well after each addition. Fold
the flour into the batter with a rubber spatula, then fold in the
boiling water.

Scrape the batter into the prepared pan and bake for about 1 hour
or until a tester inserted in the center of the cake comes out clean.
Transfer the cake to a rack set inside a rimmed baking sheet and cool
it in the pan for 10 minutes.

FOR THE GLAZE AND SERVING

Meanwhile, combine the sugar and lemon juice together in a small
saucepan. Cook, stirring, over medium-high heat for 5 minutes or
until the sugar is completely dissolved.

Invert the cake onto the rack, turn right side up, and poke it all over
with a skewer. Drizzle the glaze over the cake and allow to cool
completely, about 1 hour. Slice the cake and serve.

Makes 1 cake; serves 10 to 12

SUSIE ACHESON

{ CHEF }

Within the busy city limits of Dorset, down an obscure side street, the Deans Court property is nestled quietly behind trees. The old home, dating back to the mid-eleventh century, is a stately manor reminiscent of the kind that the Brontë sisters or Jane Austen wrote about. Ivy creeps up tall brick walls and weaves over doorframes. Ancient wood floors creak under our feet. The current owners and residents of the home, William and Ali Hanham, employ eight people, including a groundskeeper, a housekeeper, a gardener, and a cook. Deans Court is more than a home to William and Ali; it is a gathering place for festive events, a school to those willing to learn, and an oasis to all who enter.

The Hanhams run classes to teach gardening techniques and beekeeping skills. They occasionally run a tearoom and often rent out the yards for wedding receptions. Two cottages—named Apple and Plum for the orchards each overlooks respectively—have been renovated, and visitors can stay there to experience the daily existence at Deans Court. Life here is quaint indeed. The kitchen is still stocked with the chickens raised out back and the vegetables freshly picked from the abundant gardens. Daily living is quieter; brief strolls around the edge of the property are reviving. It is a life where decorum and hospitality are expected and history is rich, living, and important to the present. Deans Court is a blessed snapshot of what used to be or, at the very least, what we seem to be losing.

Susie Acheson came on as head of the kitchen only a few months before we visited. Bringing years of training and experience to the home, she has found a rhythm and comfort in the old manor. Every day, she cooks for the entire group, who sit and eat together much like a family. Lunches are served not in the formal dining room but in a cozy room off the kitchen, with high windows and even higher ceilings, dotted with collectibles and photos. Susie prepares dishes that make us feel at home—potatoes and quiches and crumbly apple cake. The group shares stories of the house, igniting our wild imaginations. We envision staying here, living in the cottages, pruning the rosebushes, and spending our days sitting by the oven with Susie, listening to her stories of world travels and delectable foods. Sadly, eventually we depart, while Deans Court stays in Dorset, welcoming visitors throughout the year. ◆

Mushroom, Tomato, and White Bean Stew

1½ tablespoons (22.5 milliliters) olive oil

2 medium onions, chopped

2 garlic cloves, minced

1 teaspoon (5 grams) dried thyme

1 teaspoon (3 grams) ground fennel seed

Pinch of dried sage

12 ounces (340 grams) cremini or baby bella mushrooms, trimmed and quartered

¼ cup (60 milliliters) chicken stock, homemade or store-bought

One 15-ounce (425-gram) can cannellini beans, drained and rinsed

One 14.5-ounce (410-gram) can petite diced tomatoes with juice

½ cup (1.6 ounces/45 grams) finely chopped flat-leaf parsley

Salt and freshly ground black pepper

Freshly grated Parmesan cheese, for serving

Heat the olive oil in a large, heavy skillet over medium-high heat until shimmering. Add the onion, garlic, thyme, fennel seed, and sage and cook, stirring occasionally, for about 8 minutes or until the onion is soft and starting to brown.

Stir in the mushrooms and stock and simmer, covered, for 5 to 6 minutes or until the mushrooms have shrunk and released their juices. Add the beans, tomatoes, and parsley, then cover and return to a simmer over medium-low heat. Simmer for 10 minutes or until slightly thickened. Season with salt and pepper to taste.

Serve hot over brown rice or whole wheat pasta, or just in a bowl as a meatless stew. Top with grated Parmesan cheese.

Serves 4

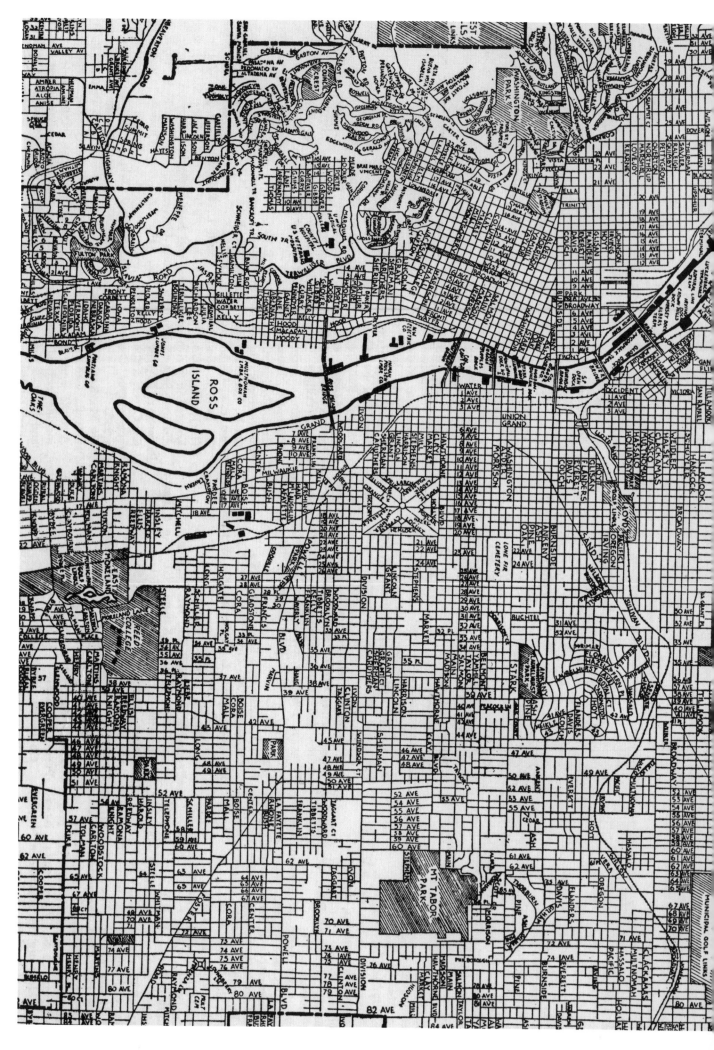

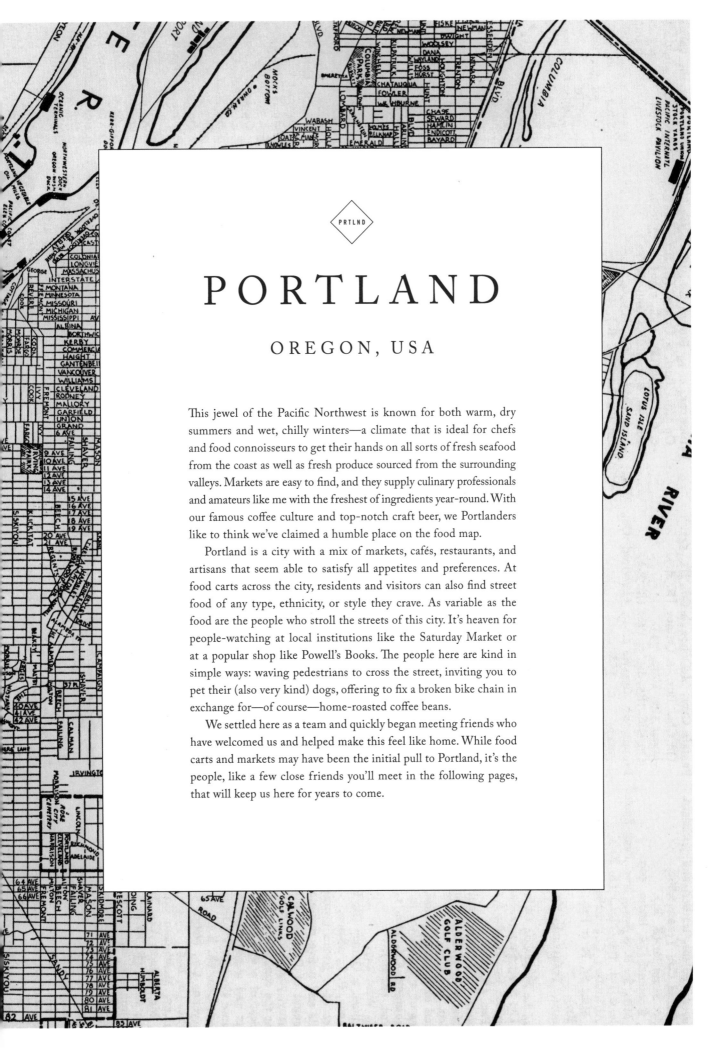

PORTLAND

OREGON, USA

This jewel of the Pacific Northwest is known for both warm, dry summers and wet, chilly winters—a climate that is ideal for chefs and food connoisseurs to get their hands on all sorts of fresh seafood from the coast as well as fresh produce sourced from the surrounding valleys. Markets are easy to find, and they supply culinary professionals and amateurs like me with the freshest of ingredients year-round. With our famous coffee culture and top-notch craft beer, we Portlanders like to think we've claimed a humble place on the food map.

Portland is a city with a mix of markets, cafés, restaurants, and artisans that seem able to satisfy all appetites and preferences. At food carts across the city, residents and visitors can also find street food of any type, ethnicity, or style they crave. As variable as the food are the people who stroll the streets of this city. It's heaven for people-watching at local institutions like the Saturday Market or at a popular shop like Powell's Books. The people here are kind in simple ways: waving pedestrians to cross the street, inviting you to pet their (also very kind) dogs, offering to fix a broken bike chain in exchange for—of course—home-roasted coffee beans.

We settled here as a team and quickly began meeting friends who have welcomed us and helped make this feel like home. While food carts and markets may have been the initial pull to Portland, it's the people, like a few close friends you'll meet in the following pages, that will keep us here for years to come.

DUSTY HUME

{ FINANCIAL ANALYST }

From the hours of nine a.m. to five p.m., Dusty Hume spends his time indoors, analyzing the performance of stocks and bonds and providing investment advice. The rest of the time, this Portland native ventures outdoors on various Oregon shore adventures, often with fortunate friends and family in tow. Dusty demonstrates the work/life balance that eludes so many of us who can't seem to step away from our desks and computers and enjoy the natural world.

He also shows us how family and food are key to creating a rhythm between our professional and personal lives. Dusty lives close to his brother, and they both remain very connected to their parents, who live just a few miles out of town. Nearly every weekend, some members of the Hume family gather along the coast to fish, forage, clam, or crab in Oregon's chilly waters. The family then takes its hard-won goods back home for nothing short of a feast. They share in the preparation, and they share their bounty. It is through these actions of foraging alongside one another, grilling together, and partaking together that this family has become so tightly woven.

One day Dusty took us to the striking Oregon shore, where he plucked mussels from their rocky homes, gathered oysters, and even caught a few crabs. He cooked us the mussels that evening in a big pot over an open flame outside, and we roasted the oysters on the grill until they gaped open. The freshness infused our mouths, and the lemony saltwater smells hung in the air. The meal was a classic study in community—eating together and eating directly from the natural world around us.

Dusty firmly believes his weekends refresh him for his workdays and his workdays give him energy and excitement for his days out. Our time with Dusty reminded us that even in the midst of busy day jobs, houses to clean, and groceries to buy, it's possible—through deliberate commitment—to pursue other things that bring us joy. He shows us that you can indeed balance work and play, and you can do it with your family by your side. ◆

Oysters on the Grill

Fresh oysters in the shell

Tabasco sauce

Lemon wedges

DUSTY: *Make two to four oysters per person unless oysters are the main course, in which case everyone will want more. It's easiest to grill about ten at a time, however, so unless you plan to stand at the grill for quite a while, you might want to make these one of several offerings at a meal.*

Heat a gas grill to medium-high according to the manufacturer's instructions.

Arrange 10 oysters convex side down on the grill and cook for 2 to 3 minutes. When the shells begin to open, use a cooking glove to steady one oyster, then gently pry it open with a shucking knife, trying to keep the oyster liquor from spilling out. Add a dash of Tabasco and a squeeze of lemon juice to the oyster. Repeat with the remaining oysters, then carefully cut the oysters from their shells, flip them over in the shells, and continue cooking for 2 to 4 minutes longer, until the flesh is firm. Serve immediately.

Steamed Mussels

4 tablespoons (2 ounces/ 60 grams) unsalted butter

2½ cups (600 milliliters) water

1 cup (240 milliliters) dry white wine

Juice of 4 lemons

1 sweet onion, such as Walla Walla, finely chopped

4 garlic cloves, chopped

½ cup (1.6 ounces/45 grams) flat-leaf parsley leaves, chopped

2 celery stalks, thinly sliced (optional)

40 mussels, scrubbed and debearded

DUSTY: *I like this dish because it isn't chemistry. Just keep testing and tasting the mixture until it tastes like the flavorful broth it should be.*

Melt the butter in a large, heavy saucepan over medium-high heat. Stir in the water, wine, and lemon juice and bring the mixture to a boil. Cook for 2 to 3 minutes or until the wine's alcoholic smell has disappeared. Stir in the onion, garlic, parsley, and celery (if using).

Stir in the mussels. If they are not completely submerged, add more water to cover them by 1 inch (2.5 centimeters). Reduce the heat to medium-low, cover, and simmer for 10 to 12 minutes or until the shells open. Serve the mussels with some of the cooking liquid.

Serves 4

ALELA DIANE MENIG

{ SINGER/SONGWRITER }

Alela Diane Menig is not of this era. Her voice, demeanor, and coiffed hair all hark back to a time many decades past—a time when women sat on farmhouse porches and collected butter dishes. She is a singer and songwriter whose music is true folk, songs that tell stories of the human condition and reveal a deep connection to place. Alela accomplishes this in both the lyrics and the melodies of her songs, and her music captures the listener because it comes from both the bitter and the sweet of life.

When she's not touring, recording, or writing new songs on her acoustic guitar, Alela lives a pretty quiet life. She is a recent cook but an esteemed and long-standing teatime hostess who counts her hours by the five or six cups of tea she steeps each day. Much like the inspiration for her songs, her nourishment comes from the land—her own garden and the many locally sourced markets around her home in Portland.

In this place where rain is king, the land is lush, spilling forth its bounty in soul-warming greenery—a welcome respite when Alela returns from traveling, staying in other people's homes and singing in dark music halls. Here at home, she wakes before dawn, makes her tea with honey, and lets the morning's quiet crawl into her farmhouse and give voice to the music through which she has so much to say to our modern world.

Almond-Coconut Granola

3 cups (10½ ounces/300 grams) whole rolled oats

1 cup (6 ounces/170 grams) whole raw almonds, coarsely chopped

½ cup (2½ ounces/70 grams) whole flaxseeds

½ cup (1¾ ounces/50 grams) unsweetened shredded coconut

½ teaspoon ground cinnamon

⅓ cup (80 milliliters) vegetable oil

⅓ cup (4 ounces/115 grams) honey

¼ cup (60 milliliters) fresh orange juice

1 teaspoon (5 milliliters) vanilla extract

ALELA: *Top with whatever suits you. I enjoy mine with banana and almond milk and a cup of English Breakfast with honey on the side. It's a perfect morning ritual.*

Position a rack in the center of the oven and preheat the oven to 300°F (150°C).

Combine the oats, almonds, flaxseeds, coconut, and cinnamon in a large bowl. Whisk the oil, honey, orange juice, and vanilla in a medium bowl. Add the oil mixture to the oat mixture and stir until thoroughly combined.

Spread the granola on a baking sheet. Bake, stirring every 15 to 20 minutes, for 45 to 60 minutes or until golden and dry. Transfer the sheet to a rack and cool completely, about 30 minutes. The granola can be stored at room temperature for up to 2 weeks and frozen for up to 4 weeks.

Makes 6 cups/500 grams

JOY &
JAY FITZGERALD

{ CALLIGRAPHER AND PHOTOGRAPHER }

Portland has become home to Jay and Joy Fitzgerald, who find inspiration amid the mountainous landscape, the creative community, and even, we daresay, the gray days. It is here that they met, connected by exploring and enjoying the city at large, and eventually fell in love. Jay is a photographer and the business partner of his brother, photographer Parker Fitzgerald; Joy is a calligrapher and illustrator. The two have carved out a life in Portland rich in friendship, family, and good food.

"My dad is the master at making simple yet delicious meals. From oatmeal to barbeque, I've learned all of the best ways to make tasty foods that are hard to mess up. Every Sunday morning before church, my dad would make a big pot of Irish oatmeal and lay out ingredients for the kids to add, and here, my love for peanut butter oatmeal was born." —JAY FITZGERALD

Joy's life, style, and tastes—food and otherwise—are all infused with the Korean traditions from her heritage, and it seems fitting that someone who finds such inspiration in her history and her family's past would make an occupation out of a seemingly lost art: calligraphy. The romanticism and legacy of hand-lettering is full of meaning for Joy, as is photography for Jay. One day Jay's brother encouraged him to pick up a camera, and in the years since he has never put it down. The natural eye behind the lens apparently runs in the family.

Although they came from very different backgrounds, Joy and Jay both attribute much of their inspiration in the kitchen and around the table to their parents. It was Joy's mother who taught her to be resourceful with what she has and to measure recipes in swigs and handfuls. It was Jay's father who taught him that simple meals, like Irish oatmeal every Sunday, are often the best of meals.

This couple has a passion for food, community, and their faith. They enjoy a rare bond, inspired by family and propelled by the mutual wish to share their friendship and their meals, generously and unconditionally. ◆

Steel-Cut Irish Oatmeal with Peanut Butter, Honey, and Cinnamon

2 cups (480 milliliters) water

½ cup (3½ ounces/100 grams) John McCann's Steel Cut Irish Oatmeal

1 tablespoon (0.56 ounce/ 15 grams) peanut butter

Honey

Ground cinnamon

Bring the water to boil in a small saucepan. Add the oatmeal and cook, stirring, until it begins to thicken. Reduce the heat to low and simmer for about 30 minutes or until thickened, stirring occasionally.

Pour the oatmeal into a bowl and stir in the peanut butter. Stir in honey and cinnamon to taste. Serve immediately.

Makes 1 serving

Spicy Fried Egg Topped with Avocado and Crumbled Feta

1 teaspoon coconut oil

1 large egg

Salt and freshly ground black pepper

½ avocado, pitted and sliced

Feta cheese, crumbled

Sriracha

Heat the oil in a small pan over medium-high heat until shimmering. Add the egg and season with salt and pepper. Cook for 3 to 6 minutes or until the egg white becomes opaque and the yolk sets to the desired doneness.

Transfer the egg to a plate, then top with the avocado and crumbled feta and sriracha to taste. Serve immediately.

Makes 1 serving

Hwe Dup Bap
(Rice Mixed with Sashimi and Greens Topped with Red Pepper Sauce)

FOR THE SAUCE

½ cup (4 ounces/115 grams) red pepper paste (go-chu-jang)

2 tablespoons (30 milliliters) white vinegar

1 tablespoon (0.42 ounces/ 13 grams) sugar

FOR THE RICE AND SASHIMI

3 cups (21 ounces/600 grams) cooked short-grain brown rice (from 1½ cups dry rice)

10 fresh perilla leaves, cut into thin strips

1 cup (1 ounce/30 grams) mixed microgreens

1 small cucumber (about 6 ounces/170 grams), seeded and thinly sliced

12 ounces (340 grams) sushi-grade raw hamachi (yellowtail), sliced ¼ inch (0.64 centimeter) thick

Dark sesame oil

FOR THE SAUCE

Combine the red pepper paste, vinegar, and sugar in a small bowl and mix until well combined.

FOR THE RICE AND SASHIMI AND ASSEMBLY

Divide the rice between two bowls. Top with the perilla leaves, microgreens, cucumber, and hamachi. Drizzle with 1 tablespoon (15 milliliters) of the sesame oil and 1 tablespoon (15 milliliters) of the sauce. Add more oil and sauce if desired. Serve with the sauce on the side or toss to combine.

Makes 2 servings

REBEKAH &
WILLE YLI-LUOMA

{ COFFEE ROASTERS/CAFÉ PROPRIETORS }

This couple could be mistaken for chemists. Rebekah and Wille Yli-Luoma are coffee connoisseurs and roasting perfectionists who concoct their brews using innovative technology coupled with stripped-down methods; the result is potentially the perfect cup.

They started a roasting company in October 2009 with the mission of bringing the best possible coffee experience to their Portland neighbors. The young company, aptly named Heart, is an abundant outpouring of Rebekah and Wille's passion for the coffee bean and its role in our daily lives. They run their company with care

"We inspire each other with ideas for cooking at home. It's fun to make up meals and discuss how we can make them even better the next time."

—WILLE YLI-LUOMA

and conviction; having caught a taste of the finest coffee they feel compelled to spread its gospel to the rest of the country.

Their small roastery now does exactly that. They ship their dark brown beans across the United States, and also serve coffee brewed from the beans fresh out of their Portland café. In three years, the couple has established a revered cup of joe, sought from near and far.

When Rebekah and Wille are at home, they spend much of their time cooking and inspiring each other in the kitchen. Wille is from Finland, and much of this couple's comfort food, like the *pulla* he expertly prepared for us, draws directly from his heritage there. This sweet, doughy bread, accompanied by a cup of coffee, holds special meaning, particularly during the Christmas holidays—a small reminder that our holiday seasons can be marked by simple joys and tastes, even in a harried time. Drinking a mug of steaming coffee, for example, need not be a rushed, on-the-go activity, but a purposeful, slow, and contemplative one. To inhale the steam and enjoy the process—this is what drinking coffee ought to be about. •

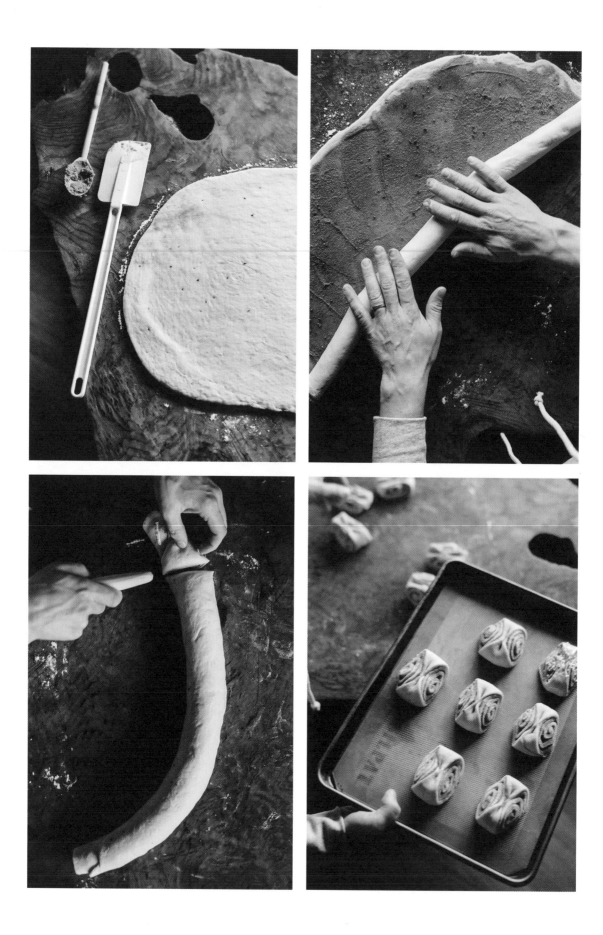

Pulla
(Finnish Dessert Bread)

FOR THE DOUGH

1¾ ounces (50 grams) fresh yeast

2 cups plus 2½ tablespoons (500 milliliters) whole milk, warmed to 95°F (35°C)

7 cups (35 ounces/1 kilogram) all-purpose flour, plus additional for dusting

1½ cups (10½ ounces/ 300 grams) granulated sugar

1 tablespoon (5 grams) cardamom seeds

1 teaspoon (6 grams) salt

12 tablespoons (6 ounces/ 170 grams) unsalted butter, softened

FOR THE FILLING

18 tablespoons (9 ounces/ 255 grams) unsalted butter, at room temperature

1 cup (7 ounces/200 grams) granulated sugar

1 tablespoon plus 2 teaspoons (15 grams) ground cinnamon

1 tablespoon (6 grams) freshly ground cardamom

1 large egg, beaten

Pearl sugar

FOR THE DOUGH

Stir the yeast and milk together in a large bowl until the yeast is completely dissolved.

Stir in the flour, sugar, cardamom, and salt and mix until combined. Stir in the butter. Knead the dough until elastic and slightly sticky, about 15 minutes, by hand, 8 minutes with an electric mixer fitted with the dough hook. Return the dough to the bowl, cover it with a dish towel, and allow it to rise in a warm, draft-free place for 1 hour or until it doubles in size.

FOR THE FILLING AND BAKING

Meanwhile, combine the butter, granulated sugar, cinnamon, and cardamom in a medium bowl and mix until thoroughly combined.

Lightly dust a clean, dry work surface with flour. Turn the risen dough out and, with a floured rolling pin, roll it out into a 20-by-16-inch (50-by-38-centimeter) rectangle about ¼ inch (0.64 centimeter) thick. Spread the filling evenly over the dough, reaching all the way to the edges, then, beginning with a long side, roll the dough into a tight cylinder. Cut the cylinder into 16 triangles. Pick up the top point of the triangle and fold it toward the center. Press the point tightly into the center.

Line two baking sheets with parchment paper and arrange eight pulla on each sheet, spacing them about 2 inches (5 centimeters) apart. Cover them with a clean dish towel and allow them to rise in a warm, draft-free place for about 1 hour or until doubled in size.

Position two racks in the upper third and lower third of the oven and preheat the oven to 400°F (204°C). Brush the pulla with the beaten egg and sprinkle them with pearl sugar. Bake for 10 to 12 minutes or until golden brown and caramelized. Serve warm.

Makes 16 pulla

Home-Brewed Coffee

0.67 ounce (19 grams) roasted coffee

9 ounces (270 milliliters) filtered water, warmed to 203°F (95°C)

WILLE: *You will need an AeroPress, AeroPress filters, a coffee grinder (use only burr grinders), an instant-read thermometer, a scale, and a mug for this recipe.*

Grind the coffee to a medium-fine grind.

Rinse a paper filter with hot water and place the coffee in the AeroPress. Add the water. Place the plunger on top of the upper chamber to stop the coffee from dripping through the filter. Allow to steep for about 2 minutes.

Remove the plunger and stir gently, then press down slowly (it should take 30 seconds).

Drink with the pulla (preceding recipe).

Makes 1 serving

RILEY MESSINA

{ FLORIST }

Some people are fortunate enough to be born into the timeless tradition of cooking and eating together. Riley Messina is one of them. Her expansive Italian-American family instilled in her the value of slow, ambling meals, best shared with the people held most dear. For Riley's family, meals were the most important activity of the day, mealtimes the most valuable hours for connecting. Today Riley carries on the family tradition in Portland, where she cooks regularly for her loved ones, always with a bottle of wine open for sharing.

A professional florist by day, Riley has filled her world with the intrinsic beauty of flowers and food. What started as a spontaneous

"Something that has always stayed with me from growing up in an Italian family is the importance of making a meal the most special part of the day. I always have sat down with my people and leisurely enjoyed dinner or whatever meal we may be sharing. Also, I always cook with a bottle of wine open and don't eat until everyone is seated." —RILEY MESSINA

apprenticeship at a florist shop has turned into an all-consuming passion. In January 2012 she opened Erba Floral, where she challenges herself to create an arrangement every day, whether the flowers are bought or foraged. Her arrangements are wild, spilling with verdant ferns and colorful buds, each reflecting and giving due respect to the wild habitat from which it sprang.

Riley's home is an oasis of greenery, vintage glassware, and beloved old kitchen items from her family. Her hours are spent slowly—drinking tea, working on puzzles, and cooking dinners. She cares little for living a flashy life, preferring to concentrate on nourishing herself and those she loves, and on the natural world around her. Deeply rooted in her family's background, she knows who she is and what she has to offer others, and she offers it with sweet generosity.

Ciabbottola

½ cup (120 milliliters) extra-virgin olive oil

4 white onions (about 2 pounds/455 grams), cut into ¼-inch (0.64-centimeter) pieces

4 green bell peppers, cut into ¼-inch (0.64-centimeter) pieces

1 red bell pepper, cut into ¼-inch (0.64-centimeter) pieces

2 pounds (910 grams) zucchini, chopped into ¼-inch (0.64-centimeter) pieces

1 eggplant (about 1½ pounds/680 grams), chopped into ¼-inch (0.64-centimeter) pieces

4 large ripe tomatoes, coarsely chopped or crushed

2 teaspoons (0.4 ounce/12 grams) sea salt

4 large eggs

Fresh basil, thinly sliced

Parmigiano-Reggiano or pecorino Romano cheese, finely grated.

RILEY: *From the Molise region of Italy,* ciabbottola *means "fills the belly" and is a rustic brunch or lunch dish. To make it even heartier, you can add fresh Italian sausage: remove it from the casings and cook in step 2 along with the onions, breaking up the pieces while cooking.*

Heat the olive oil in a large pot or Dutch oven over medium heat until shimmering.

Add the onions and green and red bell peppers and cook for 10 minutes or until the onions are soft and translucent. Stir in the zucchini, eggplant, tomatoes, and salt, then cover and reduce the heat to low. Simmer for 30 minutes.

Add the eggs and stir, gently and constantly, for about 6 minutes or until they are cooked through.

Sprinkle the *ciabbottola* with the basil and cheese. Serve.

Pictured on page 244
Serves 4

Calamari Linguini

2 large Vidalia or other sweet
onions, chopped

½ cup plus 2 tablespoons
(150 milliliters) extra-virgin
olive oil

1 pound (455 grams) cleaned
squid (about 2½), with
tentacles, cut into ½-inch
(1.28-centimeter) rings

Sea salt

3 large ripe tomatoes, coarsely
chopped or crushed

2 pounds (900 grams) linguini

Fresh basil, chopped

Hot red pepper flakes (optional)

Combine the onions and ½ cup (120 milliliters) of the olive oil in a
large pot or Dutch oven. Arrange the squid in a single layer on top
of the onions and cook, covered, over high heat for 10 minutes.

Stir in 1½ tablespoons (0.75 ounce/21 grams) salt, cover, and cook
for 15 to 20 minutes over low heat, then stir in the tomatoes and
continue cooking for 10 minutes.

Bring a large pot of water and 1 tablespoon (65 ounces/18 grams)
salt to a boil over medium-high heat. Cook the pasta just until
al dente, about 10 minutes, then drain and toss with the remaining
2 tablespoons (30 milliliters) olive oil. Transfer to a serving bowl.

Spoon the calamari over the pasta and sprinkle with basil and red
pepper flakes, if using. Serve in shallow bowls.

Serves 8

CHRIS SIEGEL &
NOLAN CALISCH

{ ORGANIC FARMERS }

Chris Siegel and Nolan Calisch are friends who share a commitment to fresh and healthy food, a commitment they have staked their lives on. The two, who met in college in Ohio, discovered their love for growing food while living in an off-the-grid housing community born as an alternative to traditional campus housing. A few years and a few states later, Nolan leased a farming property outside of Portland and Chris came running. It is here that they founded Wealth Underground Farm and brought their dream of organic farming to fruition.

For the past several years, Wealth Underground Farm has provided weekly CSA (community-supported agriculture) baskets to thirty families. This service alone keeps Chris and Nolan busy, but they don't stop their work there. Nolan freelances as a photographer and is cofounder of Farm School, a collaboration that brings together farming, art, and education. Chris is involved in the local radio scene and is the founder of the Farm to Artist media project, which provides fresh, healthy meals to touring artists. Their myriad influences and interests belie Chris and Nolan's deeper commitment to the food and art scenes at large. Both young men, who are winningly thoughtful, amiable, expressive—and incredibly hard workers—inhabit the intersection of arts that require cultivation, one from the earth and the other from the imagination. Food inspires art; art inspires food.

Chris and Nolan have created a haven for those who need to be fed and those who want to learn how to feed themselves. They grow food, cook food, and store food, and are excited to help others acquire the same skills. Their kitchen is a proverbial storehouse, especially in the winter, when all its shelves are stocked with canned and dried foods, and its freezer space is overflowing with sustenance for the season. They don't keep this bounty to themselves, however, but share it with visitors to the farm, who are always welcome to walk the grounds, spend time with the goats, and taste-test whatever happens to be in season. Essentially, Chris and Nolan are sharing the greatest wealth in this life: the wealth of fresh food, stimulating art, and creative expression, making it attainable and approachable for all. ◈

Morning Melon

1 homegrown cantaloupe or
muskmelon

Full-fat yogurt

Honey

On a warm summer morning, pick a melon from your garden, halve
it, and spoon out the seeds. Fill it with yogurt (granola, too, if you
like) and then drizzle honey over the whole deal. Sit in the sun and
eat with a spoon.

Chris's Fresh Chunky Salsa

4 medium ripe tomatoes,
chopped

1 yellow onion, chopped

½ cup (0.8 ounce/20 grams)
cilantro leaves

3 garlic cloves, minced

1 hot pepper, such as jalapeño or
Serrano, ribs and seeds removed,
chopped

1 tablespoon (15 milliliters)
white vinegar

1 tablespoon (15 milliliters)
fresh lemon juice

Salt and freshly ground black
pepper

CHRIS: *Add fresh seasonal ingredients, such as husk cherries, to this salsa
if you like.*

Reserve half of the tomatoes and onion. Pulse the remaining half of
the tomatoes and onion with the cilantro, garlic, hot pepper, vinegar,
and lemon juice in a food processor to the desired smoothness.
Stir in the reserved tomatoes and onion, season with salt and black
pepper to taste, and serve.

Makes 6 cups

ANDREW & CARISSA GALLO

{ FILMMAKER AND PHOTOGRAPHER }

This endearing couple has been a foundational part of *Kinfolk,* contributing to the publication since the release of the first issue. Andrew and Carissa Gallo produce most of the *Kinfolk* films through their production company, Sea Chant. The duo's occupation demands full creative fortitude to film, photograph, write, and design their visionary narratives. Andrew and Carissa's most cherished job, however, is raising their daughter, Rinah, and spending time together as a family, while ceaselessly welcoming friends with open doors and good meals. Their home is a refuge of sorts—a place where a casual evening dinner with friends extends into another day of sipping wine with neighbors on the back porch. While at first glance this little family may seem quiet and reserved, soon you'll find that they spend their evenings laughing at the table, dancing in the kitchen, and making music together around the piano. Their rhythm goes on and on, and plays perfectly in tune with the rest of the *Kinfolk* community. ◆

Vanilla, Lavender, and Earl Grey Chocolate Pudding with Sea Salt

1 tablespoon (0.14 ounce/ 4 grams) loose Earl Grey tea

1 tablespoon (0.07 ounce/ 2 grams) dried edible lavender flowers

¼ cup (60 milliliters) boiling water

10½ ounces (300 grams) bittersweet (60 to 70% cacao) chocolate, finely chopped

2 tablespoons (30 milliliters) vanilla extract

1 cup (240 milliliters) heavy cream

Sea salt

Lightly sweetened whipped cream

Dried edible lavender flowers

Steep the tea and lavender in the water for 5 minutes. Strain the mixture through a fine-mesh sieve into a large bowl. Press on the solids to release any liquid, then discard the solids.

Add the chocolate and vanilla to the tea mixture, stirring until the chocolate begins to melt.

Bring the cream to a boil in a small saucepan over medium-high heat and immediately pour it into the chocolate mixture, stirring until completely melted and smooth. Stir in 1½ teaspoons (9 grams) salt.

Pour the mixture into 4 to 6 ramekins or coffee cups. Press a piece of plastic wrap directly onto each of the pudding surfaces and refrigerate for about 2 hours or until chilled and set.

To serve, top with lightly sweetened whipped cream and sprinkle with dried lavender and sea salt.

Serves 4 to 6

LAURA DART

{ PHOTOGRAPHER }

Laura Dart is heard before she is seen, simply because she is always laughing. This characteristic of hers is a fitting representation of the accomplished photographer, as her jovial spirit and cheerful disposition are contagious. Laura has been contributing to *Kinfolk* since the beginning. She earned her photographic chops in Nashville, shooting musicians in the South and out on tour before she moved on to weddings and the commercial and editorial work she now primarily pursues. She enjoys great coffee in the morning and fine wine at night while she edits her work. Laura spends much of the year on the road, but her home is Portland, where she finds rest and community and makes time to work on personal projects. Laura's unabashed enthusiasm for adventure, things of beauty, and people make her an invaluable part of the *Kinfolk* family.

Sweet Potato–Mushroom Tacos with Spiced Almond Sauce

FOR THE SAUCE

1 large head of garlic

½ cup (120 milliliters) olive oil

Salt and freshly ground black pepper

¾ cup (5¼ ounces/150 grams) sliced almonds

¾ cup (3 ounces/85 grams) pumpkin seeds

1 shallot, minced

¼ teaspoon smoked paprika

¼ teaspoon ground coriander

¼ cup (60 milliliters) vegetable stock, plus additional as needed

Grated zest of 1 lemon

¼ cup (60 milliliters) canola oil

FOR THE SAUCE

Position a rack in the center of the oven and preheat the oven to 400°F (204°C). Cut the garlic in half, drizzle it with 3 tablespoons (45 milliliters) of the olive oil, and season the cut sides with salt. Press the garlic halves together, wrap them in foil, and roast for 1 hour or until the cloves are golden and soft. Transfer the foil packet to a rack; reserve. Turn off the oven.

Combine the almonds and pumpkin seeds in a medium bowl and add enough boiling water to cover by 1 inch (2.5 centimeters). Allow to soak for 10 minutes, then drain.

Heat 1 tablespoon (15 milliliters) olive oil in a small skillet over medium-high heat until shimmering. Cook the shallot, paprika, coriander, and a pinch of salt for 5 minutes, stirring occasionally, or until the shallot mixture is soft and translucent. Transfer the shallot mixture to a food processor.

Squeeze the garlic from the skin into the food processor. Add the almonds, pumpkin seeds, vegetable stock, and lemon zest and pulse until the mixture is creamy. With the mixer running, pour the remaining ¼ cup (60 milliliters) olive oil and the canola oil through the feed tube and continue to process until the oils are completely incorporated. Season with salt and pepper; reserve.

FOR THE TACOS

2 sweet potatoes (about 22 ounces/620 grams), scrubbed and cut into ½-inch (1.28-centimeter) pieces

Large pinch of ground cinnamon

Large pinch of ground cumin

Pinch of cayenne

¼ cup (60 milliliters) olive oil

Salt and freshly ground black pepper

1 tablespoon (0.5 ounce/ 14 grams) unsalted butter

10 ounces (280 grams) mushrooms, such as cremini or shiitake, cleaned and sliced

3 garlic cloves, minced

1½ cups (1½ ounces/45 grams) flat-leaf parsley, chopped

Twelve 6-inch (15.24-centimeter) corn tortillas

Cilantro leaves

Pumpkin seeds, chopped

FOR THE TACOS

Position a rack in the center of the oven and preheat the oven to 400°F (204°C).

Toss the sweet potatoes with the cinnamon, cumin, and cayenne on a foil-lined baking sheet. Drizzle them with 3 tablespoons (45 milliliters) of the olive oil and season with salt and pepper. Cook for 40 minutes or until tender. Transfer to a rack and cover loosely with foil.

Melt the butter in a large skillet over medium-high heat. Add the remaining 1 tablespoon (15 milliliters) olive oil and the mushrooms and season with salt and pepper. Cook for about 3 minutes, stirring occasionally, or until the mushrooms begin to release liquid. Stir in the garlic and continue cooking, stirring occasionally, for about 5 minutes or until the mushrooms are golden. Stir in the parsley and remove from the heat.

Cook the tortillas directly on the stovetop flame for 30 seconds per side. Wrap them in a clean dish towel to keep them warm. Alternatively, heat a large skillet over medium-high heat and cook the tortillas for 1 minute per side or until warmed through and slightly crisped.

To assemble the tacos, fill each tortilla with sweet potatoes and mushrooms, then top with cilantro leaves and pumpkin seeds. Serve with the spiced almond sauce.

Pictured on page 261
Serves 4

DOUG & PAIGE BISCHOFF

{ ENTREPRENEURS }

Doug and Paige Bischoff are a silent force behind the operations of *Kinfolk,* handling the distribution and accounting, respectively. This pair's keen skills are almost as valuable as their affable companionship, and their son, Porter, is perhaps the most sought-after little man within the *Kinfolk* circle of friends. Doug and Paige are always gracious, as hosts or guests alike. Their easygoing personalities make for natural, laid-back relationships, and they frequently spend hours over a simple meal with friends. They appreciate well-made food but are just as content with a low-key gathering involving lounging around and snacking on this and that. Whenever we're with the Bischoffs, they laugh uproariously and laud the food, no matter what it is. They hold nothing back in their affections, and are always at the ready to serve others, which might make them a host's favorite guest. They are vital in the day-to-day community of *Kinfolk* for both their joy and their wisdom. ◆

Rosemary Garlic Bread

1 large head of garlic

½ cup (120 milliliters) extra-virgin olive oil, plus additional for brushing and serving

Salt

2 teaspoons (0.16 ounce/ 4.6 grams) sugar

1½ teaspoons (0.19 ounce/ 5.5 grams) active dry yeast

1 cup (240 milliliters) water, warmed to 110°F (43°C)

3 to 4 cups (18 to 24 ounce/ 510 to 680 grams) wheat (bread) flour

2 tablespoons (6 grams) minced fresh rosemary

½ teaspoon dried oregano

Freshly ground black pepper

Coarse sea salt

Balsamic vinegar

DOUG & PAIGE: *Serve this bread fresh and warm, with your favorite blend of good olive oil, freshly ground black pepper, and balsamic vinegar.*

Position a rack in the center of the oven and preheat the oven to 400°F (204°C). Cut the garlic in half, drizzle it with 3 tablespoons (45 milliliters) of the olive oil, and season the cut sides with salt. Press the garlic halves together, wrap them in foil, and roast for 1 hour or until the cloves are golden and soft. Transfer the foil packet to a rack; reserve. Turn off the oven.

Combine the sugar and 2 teaspoons (12 grams) salt in a large bowl. Stir in the yeast and water and allow the mixture to stand until it foams, about 10 minutes. Stir in 3 tablespoons (45 milliliters) olive oil and 3 cups (510 grams) of the flour. Turn the mixture out onto a clean work surface and knead the dough for about 10 minutes or until elastic and slightly sticky. (If using a stand mixer, fit it with the dough hook and knead the dough on medium speed for about 6 minutes, until it is elastic and slightly sticky.) If the dough is too sticky, add more flour, 2 tablespoons (18 grams) at a time, kneading in between additions.

Add 1 tablespoon (3 grams) rosemary, the oregano, and ¼ teaspoon pepper, then knead for another 5 minutes. Squeeze the cloves out of the garlic skin and gently knead them into the dough for about 1 minute or until combined. Shape the dough into a ball. Brush a large bowl with the remaining 2 tablespoons (30 milliliters) olive oil, place the dough inside, and turn it over several times until coated with oil. Cover the bowl tightly with plastic wrap and allow the dough to rise in a warm, draft-free place for 1 hour or until doubled in size.

After the dough has risen, punch it down and shape it into a round loaf. Using a sharp knife, make a crisscross design on top. Place the loaf on an oiled baking sheet, then cover it with a large bowl. Allow the dough to rise in a warm, draft-free place for 1 hour or until doubled in size.

Preheat the oven to 375°F (190°C). Brush the loaf lightly with olive oil, then sprinkle it with the sea salt and the remaining 1 tablespoon (3 grams) rosemary. Bake for 15 minutes, then spray the loaf with water and continue baking for 15 minutes. Increase the oven temperature to 425°F (218°C), spray the loaf with water once again, and bake for 5 minutes longer or just until the top is golden brown. Transfer the baking sheet to a rack and cool for 10 minutes. Serve with olive oil, balsamic vinegar, and pepper. The bread is best eaten the day it is made.

Note: You'll need a spray bottle filled with water for this recipe.

Makes 1 loaf

JULIE POINTER

{ CURATOR }

Julie Pointer is a soft-spoken gem of Portland, and her home could be the symbolic representation of all that is simple and true about hospitality. She herself is a most natural hostess. She does not stress or complicate a gathering. She keeps her guests at ease by being at ease herself. She floats as she refills glasses, stokes the fire, or checks on the pie. She hosts from a restful and wise anticipation of the needs of both the guests and the surrounding environment to make a gathering truly intimate and authentically connecting.

Julie is making a life from her innate gift for hospitality. After graduating with a master of fine arts degree in applied craft and design, she found a natural fit working with our team to envision and develop our community events, starting with a series of dinners held mostly around the United States and Canada. Julie is the quality control of these occasions, ensuring that each shared environment not only is memorable but also fosters a spirit of community and creates a safe, inviting space for meaningful conversation around an abundance of wholesome foods. She has worked tirelessly to design and execute these gatherings for the advocates and supporters of *Kinfolk*'s simple approach to hospitality. She encourages readers and guests to attend the dinners closest to where they live and partners exclusively with local businesses; as a result, each gathering seems to be a distinct representation of the people, the culture, and the location in which it is held. From the initial series of meandering meals, these communal gatherings have become greater than the sum of their parts. These evenings, spent with friends new and old around a table, represent snapshots of a culture and place. ◆

Sweet Potato–Apple Salad

FOR THE SALAD

1 sweet potato (about
11 ounces/310 grams), scrubbed
and sliced crosswise ¼ inch
(0.64 centimeter) thick

3 tablespoons (45 milliliters)
olive oil

3 tablespoons (45 milliliters)
pure maple syrup

1 teaspoon (3 grams) ground
cinnamon

Coarse sea salt and freshly
ground black pepper

½ yellow onion, sliced ¼ inch
(0.64 centimeter) thick

FOR THE DRESSING

1½ tablespoons (22.5 milliliters)
olive oil

Juice of ½ lemon

1 garlic clove, minced

Honey

Coarse sea salt and freshly
ground black pepper

4 cups (4 ounces/115 grams)
mixed salad greens, spinach, or
kale

1 apple, cored and sliced ¼ inch
(0.64 centimeter) thick

¼ cup (1 ounce/30 grams)
walnuts, chopped

¼ cup (1 ounce/30 grams)
pecans, chopped

¼ cup (1 ounce/30 grams)
roasted pumpkin seeds

6 ounces (170 grams) goat
cheese, crumbled

Position a rack in the center of the oven and preheat the oven to
375°F (190°C).

Toss the sweet potato slices with 2 tablespoons (30 milliliters) of the
olive oil, 2 tablespoons (30 milliliters) of the maple syrup, and the
cinnamon on a foil-lined baking sheet. Season with salt and pepper.

Roast for about 40 minutes or until tender and golden, turning the
potatoes over halfway through the cooking time. Transfer the sheet
to a rack and cool the potatoes for about 15 minutes.

Meanwhile, heat the remaining 1 tablespoon (15 milliliters) olive
oil in a large skillet over medium-high heat until shimmering. Add
the onion and the remaining 1 tablespoon (15 milliliters) syrup and
cook, stirring occasionally, for 5 to 7 minutes or until softened and
caramelized.

FOR THE DRESSING AND ASSEMBLY

Whisk the olive oil, lemon juice, garlic, and 1 teaspoon (7 grams)
honey together in a small bowl. Season with salt, pepper, and
additional honey to taste.

Toss the greens, apple slices, sweet potatoes, onions, nuts, seeds, and
cheese together in a salad bowl. Season with salt and pepper to taste.
Add the dressing and toss to coat. Serve.

Notes: Turn this salad into a heftier dish by mixing in slices of
cooked chicken. To maximize flavor, add the chicken to the skillet
after the onions have been cooked.

For a heftier but still vegetarian salad, serve with cooked quinoa.

Serves 2

Oatmeal Chocolate Chip Cookies

Adapted from Annie's
Oatmeal Cookies

1 cup (8 ounces/230 grams)
packed dark brown sugar

1 cup (7 ounces/200 grams)
granulated sugar

1 cup (8 ounces/230 grams)
organic vegetable shortening, at
room temperature

1 teaspoon (5 milliliters) vanilla
extract

1 teaspoon (6 grams) salt

1 teaspoon (3 grams) baking
soda

2 large eggs, beaten and at room
temperature

1½ cups (7½ ounces/210 grams)
all-purpose flour

3 cups (10½ ounces/300 grams)
whole rolled oats

1 cup (12 ounces/340 grams)
semisweet or bittersweet
chocolate chips

Combine the sugars and shortening in a large bowl and mix until smooth and creamy. Add the vanilla, salt, baking soda, and eggs and mix until just combined.

Stir in the flour, oats, and chocolate chips. Cover the bowl with plastic wrap and refrigerate for about 1 hour or until the dough is chilled and firm.

Position a rack in the center of the oven and preheat the oven to 350°F (177°C). Line two baking sheets with parchment paper.

Using a small ice cream scoop with a release mechanism or a 2-tablespoon (30-milliliter) measure, scoop the dough out into balls and place them on the prepared baking sheets about 1 inch (2.5 centimeters) apart. Press the dough down gently with your fingertips.

Bake for 10 to 12 minutes, rotating and alternating the sheets halfway through the baking time, until the cookie edges begin to brown. Immediately remove the sheets from the oven and rap them sharply on a counter.

Transfer the sheets to a rack and cool the cookies on the sheets for 5 minutes. With a spatula, transfer the cookies to the rack and cool completely, about 30 minutes. Serve or store in an airtight container for up to 3 days.

Notes: The organic shortening may be replaced with a blend of equal amounts of organic shortening and butter. Do not replace the full amount of shortening with butter as it will alter the cookies' texture.

Half a cup of the all-purpose flour may be replaced with ½ cup whole wheat flour.

Mixing the dough by hand is a must—using an electric mixer changes the consistency of these cookies.

Makes about 3 dozen cookies

"Everyone knows I have an insatiable sweet tooth—so while I love baking and making sweet things, I've now gotten in the habit of giving away most of the things I make. Otherwise I might enjoy them all myself! Thankfully I know most of my neighbors, so I have lots of willing recipients within close reach. I have a friend who refers to me as a little bear cub with my paws always in the honey pot; the comparison unfortunately rings quite true."

—JULIE POINTER

PORTLAND, OREGON, USA

SUZANNE FUOCO

{ JAM MAKER }

If Suzanne Fuoco could be described in colors, she would be the yellow of a Meyer lemon or the red of a ripe raspberry. Her personality is as bright as the natural world around her. She is the effusive and inspiring woman behind Pink Slip Jams, a madly popular company selling, as she says, "naked jams, potions, and so on." Her life and style are multilayered, steeped in history and tradition, though accented with plenty of quirks.

Suzanne's various jams, chutneys, and syrups were born of her grandmother's legacy, juxtaposed with a genuine appreciation for fresh food and the farmers who make it. After relocating to the

---

"I hope I have succeeded in being a good role model for generosity for our kids; whether it's around the table, offering food from our garden, or just extending help in making a meal." —SUZANNE FUOCO

Portland region several years ago from Berkeley, California, Suzanne traded her year-round citrus for the bounty of Northwest berries, and thus began her foray into preserves. She uses only the best unadulterated, organic fruits and sugars, so her concoctions possess the truest of flavors.

During the week, Suzanne works as a school nurse, a job that she believes gives her a great opportunity to talk to children about healthy eating habits. Besides her work at the school and her work making jams, she is the mother to three rambunctious sons, who together hold the coveted position of official taste tester. Suzanne's world might bubble with jams and preserves, but her family is the foundation. Imparting her belief in the importance of real foods to the younger generations is her chief concern. She models intentional eating, cooking, and sourcing with the hope that her sons will follow her ethic and embrace her beliefs. ◆

Sir Isaac's Folly
(Spiced Apple Chutney)

1 cup (240 milliliters) apple cider vinegar

6 baking apples, peeled, cored, and cut into ½-inch (1.28-centimeter) pieces (see Notes)

2 cups (16 ounces/455 grams) packed light brown sugar

1 yellow onion, finely chopped

1 cup (5 ounces/142 grams) dried cranberries or golden raisins (see Notes)

2 ounces (60 grams) fresh ginger, peeled and grated

3 garlic cloves, minced

1 tablespoon (0.35 ounce/ 10 grams) black mustard seeds

2 teaspoons (0.2 ounce/6 grams) mild curry powder

1 teaspoon (0.2 ounce/6 grams) salt

1 teaspoon (0.1 ounce/3 grams) ground allspice

Combine the vinegar, apples, sugar, onion, cranberries, ginger, and garlic in a large saucepan and bring to a boil over medium-high heat, stirring constantly. Reduce the heat to medium-low and simmer for 30 to 35 minutes or until the apples are softened, stirring occasionally.

Stir in the mustard seeds, curry powder, salt, and allspice and simmer for 15 minutes, stirring occasionally.

The chutney may be refrigerated in an airtight container and stored for up to 3 weeks. Alternatively, spoon the chutney into sterilized ½-cup (120-milliliter) pickling jars and process them for longer storage, up to 1 year.

Notes: To prevent the apples from oxidizing, first pour the vinegar into the saucepan and add the apples as soon as you dice them.

You can use a combination of dried cranberries and golden raisins in this recipe.

Makes about 3 cups/710 milliliters

Roasted Pork Loin and Apple Chutney

Two 1- to 1¼-pound (455- to 570-gram) pork tenderloins

½ cup (120 milliliters) apple cider

½ cup (120 milliliters) dry red or white wine

1 cup (240 milliliters) Sir Isaac's Folly apple chutney (preceding recipe)

4 garlic cloves, chopped

2 tablespoons (0.2 ounce/ 5 grams) fresh thyme leaves, plus additional for garnish

Salt and freshly ground black pepper

3 tablespoons (45 milliliters) olive oil

SUZANNE: *This is a great autumn meal served with mashed sweet potatoes or yams and a green salad with pears—and it's pretty too!*

Rinse the pork and pat dry thoroughly with paper towels. Arrange the tenderloins in a shallow baking pan.

Stir the cider, wine, chutney, garlic, and thyme together and pour the mixture over the pork. Cover the pan with plastic wrap and allow to marinate at room temperature for at least 1 hour and up to 3 hours.

Position a rack in the center of the oven and preheat the oven to 375°F (190°C).

Remove the pork from the marinade (reserve the marinade) and season with salt and pepper. Heat the olive oil in a large skillet or Dutch oven over medium-high heat until just smoking. Cook the tenderloins for about 6 minutes or until well browned on all sides.

Pour the reserved marinade over the pork and transfer to the oven. Roast, basting occasionally, for about 20 minutes or until an instant-read thermometer inserted in the thickest part of the tenderloins registers 145°F (63°C) for medium doneness. Transfer the pork to a cutting board, cover loosely with foil, and allow to rest for 5 minutes. Slice the pork and serve with the pan juices. Garnish with thyme sprigs.

Serves 6

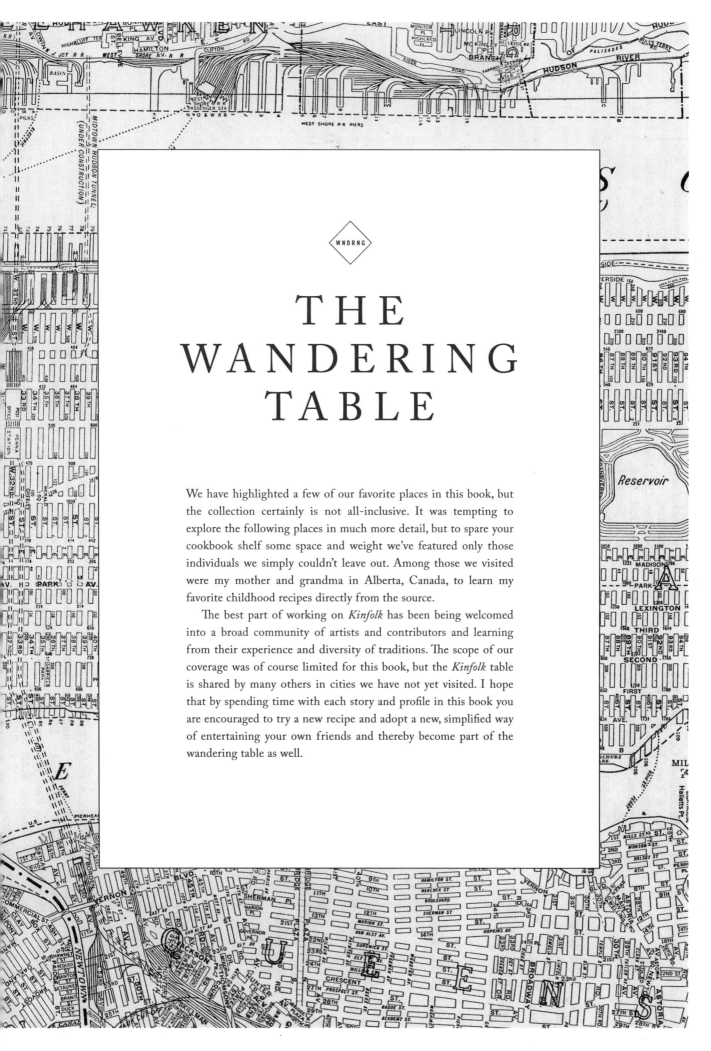

THE WANDERING TABLE

We have highlighted a few of our favorite places in this book, but the collection certainly is not all-inclusive. It was tempting to explore the following places in much more detail, but to spare your cookbook shelf some space and weight we've featured only those individuals we simply couldn't leave out. Among those we visited were my mother and grandma in Alberta, Canada, to learn my favorite childhood recipes directly from the source.

The best part of working on *Kinfolk* has been being welcomed into a broad community of artists and contributors and learning from their experience and diversity of traditions. The scope of our coverage was of course limited for this book, but the *Kinfolk* table is shared by many others in cities we have not yet visited. I hope that by spending time with each story and profile in this book you are encouraged to try a new recipe and adopt a new, simplified way of entertaining your own friends and thereby become part of the wandering table as well.

SARAH &
DAVID WINWARD

{ FLORIST AND LAW OFFICE MANAGER }
SALT LAKE CITY, UTAH

Sarah's flowers are everywhere; her arrangements have graced our quarterly pages and our dinner tables and have been depicted across the virtual world. They are bold, earthy, and wildly stunning, much like Sarah herself. Her creations are, simply put, works of art, and are treated as such by those who enjoy them.

Sarah, David, and Ivy Winward live in the Canyon Rim region of Salt Lake City; their quiet neighborhood abuts stark mountains and ridgelines. Sarah's floral boutique, Honey of a Thousand Flowers, is situated in a small studio in the city, where she spends most of her time when not out on location at weddings or special events. David passes his daytime hours managing a law office and in the evening hours unwinds by engaging in his own creative pursuits, such as sketching, knitting, and writing. Often the couple hosts friends for meals that last for hours, moving from their outdoor table softly lit by hanging bulbs to the adjacent fire pit, where they sit and talk some more. Sarah's elegantly unruly backyard garden beckons guests to wander through the foliage and make friends with her bees, while David's soft, attentive demeanor keeps company content to chat late into the night.

David and Sarah are collectors of vintage china sets and antique dishware and flatware, and these pieces, acquired one by one, fill their carefully curated cabinets and drawers to create a united aesthetic that is vintage, natural, simple, and clean. Sarah's grandmother's cast-iron sauce pot is one example of the items they treasure. They use it almost daily and hold steadfast to the claim that it has never burned a sauce. The pot is an apt parallel for this young family, who are deeply rooted in tradition, bent on carrying on their extended family's love of food and time spent together around the table to the next generation, starting with young Ivy. With a great sauce pot come great meals and memorable nights enjoying them with friends. ◆

Winter Wilted Greens and Potato Soup

3 tablespoons (45 milliliters) olive oil

1 yellow onion, thinly sliced

6 cups (1.4 liters) vegetable stock

2 garlic cloves, minced

1 pound (455 grams) red potatoes, scrubbed and cut into ½-inch (1.28-centimeter) pieces

1 small bunch of fresh dill, chopped

Salt and freshly ground black pepper

3 red chard leaves, torn into small pieces

3 lacinato kale leaves, torn into small pieces

2 cups (about 12 ounces/ 340 grams) shredded cooked chicken (optional)

Juice of ½ lemon

Heat 2 tablespoons (30 milliliters) of the olive oil in a large pot or Dutch oven over medium heat until shimmering. Add the onion and cook, stirring and adding small amounts of the stock to help steam the onion, for 5 minutes or until the onion is soft and translucent. Add the garlic and cook, stirring, for 1 minute or until fragrant.

Stir in the remaining stock, the potatoes, dill, 1 teaspoon (6 grams) salt, and ½ teaspoon pepper, and simmer over medium-low heat until just tender.

Heat the remaining 1 tablespoon (15 milliliters) olive oil in a medium skillet over medium heat until shimmering. Add the chard and kale and cook, stirring, for about 3 minutes or until wilted. Stir them into the pot.

Add the chicken, if using, and heat through, then season the soup with salt and pepper to taste and add the lemon juice. Serve.

Serves 4

Summer Squash and Tomato Salad

3 tablespoons (45 milliliters) extra-virgin olive oil

3 summer squash (about 24 ounces/680 grams), sliced lengthwise ¼ inch (0.64 centimeter) thick (see Note)

1 tablespoon (0.1 ounce/ 3 grams) fresh thyme leaves

Salt and freshly ground black pepper

Kernels from 1 ear corn

2 radishes, sliced ⅛ inch (0.32 centimeter) thick (see Note)

3 cups cherry tomatoes (about 3 ounces/90 grams), halved

4 cups (4 ounces/115 grams) arugula

1 cup (2 ounces/60 grams) shaved pecorino Romano cheese

Balsamic vinegar (optional)

Light salad dressing of choice (optional)

Heat 2 tablespoons (30 milliliters) of the olive oil in a large skillet over medium-high heat until shimmering. Cook the squash, stirring carefully, adding the thyme and seasoning with salt and pepper, for 3 to 4 minutes or until tender. Transfer the squash to a salad bowl.

Heat the remaining 1 tablespoon (15 milliliters) olive oil in the skillet over medium-high heat until shimmering. Add the corn and season with salt and pepper. Cook, stirring occasionally, for 3 to 4 minutes or until tender and beginning to brown. Scrape the corn into the salad bowl.

Add the radishes, tomatoes, arugula, and cheese to the salad bowl and toss gently to combine, being careful not to tear the squash ribbons. Drizzle with balsamic vinegar or dressing if desired. Serve.

Note: A mandoline is the most efficient tool for thinly slicing vegetables. If you don't have one, use a very sharp chef's knife.

Serves 4 to 6 as a side dish

VERA WILLIAMS

{ MOTHER/HOME COOK }
MAGRATH, ALBERTA, CANADA

Vera is my mother. In fact, I consider her the quintessential mother, her life's work unfolding in the space where she takes care of our family, in a home where she keeps the front door unconditionally open. My mom lives in a small town in Alberta, Canada, where she keeps her days busy with grandchildren, baking, hosting friends, and battling deer to protect her garden vegetables. She has built a home where her kids, including me, have enjoyed spending their time—in their childhood and adolescence, and even now as adults.

She has always been aggressive with her "sugar-flour-butter" tactics, designed to win the hearts and appetites of any visitors that come to the house, and accordingly, the kitchen can always be trusted to have warm cookies, soups, or rolls ready for the taking. Although healthy, fresh-from-the-garden meals are also part of her repertoire, she is not afraid to liberally use heavy cream, butter, and sugar, and I have never complained.

To this day, my mom still mails us—her children near and far—parcels of cookies wrapped and padded in tissue paper, and the rest of the *Kinfolk* team has been the happy recipients of some of those leftovers. Although the treats often arrive in crumbles and broken pieces, the act remains a symbol of the time she invests in those that she loves. It seems that her special parcels have served her well; she is beloved and revered by all of us, and regarded as a mother to many more than just those she raised in our home. ◆

Vera's Buns

1½ tablespoons (0.6 ounce/
16.5 grams) active dry yeast

2½ cups (600 milliliters) water,
warmed to 110°F/45°C

½ cup plus ½ teaspoon
(7 ounces/102 grams) sugar

3 tablespoons (45 milliliters)
vegetable oil

1½ teaspoons (9 grams) salt

5 cups (25 ounces/710 grams)
all-purpose flour, plus additional
for mixing the dough

VERA: *I worked at perfecting a bun recipe years ago, and now I am known for "Vera's Buns." I am asked to bring my buns to every event or dinner we are invited to. I have taught many bun classes to women who want to know how I make them. I share my recipe often and am asked by friends if they can come over and watch the process. The joke in our extended family gatherings is that everyone loves Vera's Buns. I am always flattered. It never gets old.*

Stir the yeast, ½ cup (120 milliliters) of the water, and ½ teaspoon of the sugar together in a small bowl and allow the mixture to stand until it foams, about 10 minutes.

Fit a stand mixer with the dough hook. In the bowl of the stand mixer, stir together the remaining 2 cups (480 milliliters) water, the remaining ½ cup (100 grams) sugar, the oil, and the salt until the sugar is completely dissolved. Add 2 cups (480 grams) of the flour and mix on low speed until just incorporated. Add the yeast mixture and continue mixing until combined.

Add the remaining 3 cups (426 grams) flour, ½ cup (71 grams) at a time, mixing to incorporate between additions. Increase the mixer speed to medium and knead for 6 to 8 minutes or until the dough is elastic and slightly sticky. The dough should pull away from the sides of the bowl; if it does not, add more flour, 2 tablespoons (18 grams) at a time.

Shape the dough into a ball, return it to the bowl, cover it with a dish towel, and allow it to rise in a warm, draft-free place for about 1 hour or until it doubles in size.

Punch down the dough and move it to a work surface. Cut the dough into 2-inch (5-centimeter) pieces and shape them between your palms to form balls. Arrange them about 2 inches (5 centimeters) apart on two baking sheets, cover them with clean dish towels, and allow them to rise in a warm, draft-free place for about 1 hour or until they double in size.

Position a rack in the upper third of the oven and one in the lower third and preheat the oven to 350°F (177°C). Bake the buns for about 20 minutes or until golden, rotating and alternating the sheets halfway through the baking time. Transfer the sheets to racks and cool the buns for about 10 minutes. Serve. The buns can be stored in an airtight container for 3 or 4 days or frozen for up to 1 month. Reheat in a 350°F/177°C oven.

Makes 20 to 24 buns

Almond Sugar Cookies

FOR THE COOKIES

6 cups (30 ounces/850 grams) all-purpose flour, plus additional for dusting

2 tablespoons (0.6 ounce/ 6 grams) baking powder

1 teaspoon (0.2 ounce/6 grams) salt

2 cups (4 sticks/455 grams) unsalted butter, at room temperature

2 cups (14 ounces/400 grams) sugar

4 large eggs

½ cup (120 milliliters) milk

2 teaspoons (0.3 ounce/ 10 milliliters) almond extract

FOR THE COOKIES

Position a rack in the upper third of the oven and one in the lower third and preheat the oven to 350°F (177°C).

Mix the flour, baking powder, and salt in a bowl and set aside.

Beat the butter and sugar in a large bowl with an electric mixer on medium-high speed until light and fluffy, about 2 minutes. Add the eggs, one at a time, beating well after each addition. Scrape down the sides of the bowl with a rubber spatula as needed. Combine the milk and almond extract in a liquid measuring cup.

Reduce the mixer speed to low and add the flour mixture in three additions, alternating with the milk. Gather the dough into two balls, wrap them in plastic wrap, and refrigerate for 1 hour or until thoroughly chilled.

Lightly dust a clean, dry work surface with flour. Working with one ball of dough at a time, roll out the dough ¼ inch (0.63 centimeter) thick. Stamp out cookies with a 2-inch (5-centimeter) cookie cutter or drinking glass. Alternatively, stamp the dough out with decorative cookie cutters.

Line two baking sheets or cookie sheets with parchment paper. Arrange the cookies on the prepared sheets, about 1½ inches (3.8 centimeters) apart. Bake for 8 to 10 minutes, rotating and alternating the sheets halfway through the baking time, or until the edges begin to turn golden. Transfer the sheets to racks and cool on the sheets for 5 minutes. With a spatula, transfer the cookies to the racks and cool completely, about 1 hour.

Repeat the baking procedure with the remaining dough. The cooled cookies may be stored in an airtight container at room temperature for up to 3 days or in the freezer for up to 1 month.

FOR THE ICING

3 cups (12½ ounces/360 grams)
confectioners' sugar

4 ounces (115 grams) cream
cheese, at room temperature

4 tablespoons (2 ounces/
60 grams) unsalted butter, at
room temperature

1 teaspoon (5 milliliters)
almond extract

Whole milk, as needed

FOR THE ICING

Beat the confectioners' sugar, cream cheese, butter, and almond extract in a bowl with an electric mixer on low speed until combined. Increase the speed to medium and beat until light and fluffy, about 3 minutes. Whisk in the milk 1 tablespoon (15 milliliters) at a time until the consistency is spreadable.

Spread the icing on the cooled cookies with a small offset spatula or the back of a teaspoon. Allow to set for 10 minutes and serve.

Makes about 80 cookies

ALICE GAO

{ PHOTOGRAPHER }

NEW YORK, NEW YORK

Alice Gao made the giant leap from economics and consumer psychology to full-time photography a few years ago, and she hasn't looked back. She dabbles in a spectrum of projects—including portraits, food, weddings, interiors, and the occasional travelogue. Her photographs speak volumes and tell long stories.

Alice's still shots are crisp and lush, her colors warm and inviting. She captures personalities with astute clarity, and her still lifes are more reminiscent of renaissance paintings than of digital creations.

"I think I've always just loved details, whether in visual imagery or in literature, and seeing beauty in everyday objects. I love the whole game of light and composition, and the idea of immortalizing a fleeting moment through a camera's lens." —ALICE GAO

Preoccupied with details, she finds the frame and from there balances light and composition until each picture is perfect.

Her photographs may draw unassuming outsiders into her world, but it's Alice's warmth and approachability that keep people there. When she welcomed us into her cozy apartment in the South Street Seaport area of Manhattan with strong, smooth coffee and crumbly scones, the aromas alone were enough. Although she claims she's not an expert in the kitchen, the sincerity with which she welcomed us and the artistry with which she served us revealed her to be a comforting hostess with a keen eye. ◆

Tea-Smoked Eggs

12 large eggs

Two 8-inch (20-centimeter) square sheets dried lotus leaves (about 0.42 ounce/ 12 grams)

3 star anise pods

One cinnamon stick

2 tablespoons (30 milliliters) dark soy sauce

1 tablespoon (0.6 ounce/ 18 grams) salt

Place the eggs in a large saucepan and add enough water to cover by 2 inches (5 centimeters), bring to a boil over medium-high heat, and cook for 1 minute. Remove the pan from the heat and allow the eggs to sit for 10 minutes.

Remove the eggs from the pan with a slotted spoon and reserve the water. Gently crack the shells all over with the back of a spoon.

Push one of the lotus leaves to the bottom of the pan with a cooking spoon, than add the star anise, cinnamon, soy sauce, and salt. Return the eggs to the pan and cover with the remaining lotus leaf. Bring the eggs to a boil over medium-high heat, then reduce the heat to low and simmer for 45 minutes.

Cool the water and eggs to room temperature, then refrigerate until thoroughly chilled, at least 8 hours. Peel the eggs and serve.

Makes 1 dozen eggs

Blueberry Scones

Recipe adapted from Martha Stewart

2 cups (10 ounces/280 grams) all-purpose flour, plus additional for dusting

3 tablespoons (1.3 ounces/ 38 grams) sugar, plus additional for sprinkling

1 tablespoon (0.3 ounce/ 9 grams) baking powder

½ teaspoon salt

¼ cup plus 2 tablespoons (3 ounces/90 grams) unsalted butter, cut into small pieces and chilled

1 cup (5½ ounces/160 grams) fresh blueberries

Grated zest of 1 lemon

2 large eggs

⅓ cup (80 milliliters) heavy cream, plus additional for brushing

½ teaspoon vanilla extract

Position a rack in the center of the oven and preheat the oven to 400°F (204°C).

Sift the flour, sugar, baking powder, and salt into a large bowl. Using two knives, cut the butter into the flour mixture until it resembles small peas. Stir in the blueberries and lemon zest.

Whisk the eggs in a liquid measuring cup until well beaten, then whisk in the cream and vanilla.

Stir the egg mixture into the flour mixture with a fork, mixing just until combined. The mixture should look shaggy.

Lightly dust a clean, dry work surface with flour. Turn the dough out and knead it just until combined. Shape the dough into a 6-inch (15-centimeter) square. Cut the dough into four 3-inch (7.5-centimeter) squares, then cut the squares diagonally into eight triangles.

Arrange the scones on a parchment-paper-lined baking sheet. Brush the tops with cream and sprinkle them with sugar.

Bake for 16 to 18 minutes or until the tops are golden brown. Transfer the sheet to a rack and cool for about 5 minutes. Serve warm.

Pictured on page 301
Makes 8 scones

ATHENA CALDERONE

{ INTERIOR DESIGNER }
AMAGANSETT, NEW YORK

When you're looking for a home, the standard reaction to a house that has black mold crawling up its walls and rooms infested with mosquitoes is to run the other way. Unless you are Athena Calderone, who can conjure up a vision for even the most challenging of spaces. The Calderone home in Amagansett, New York, is a testament to Athena's imagination and skill as an interior designer—a decrepit house transformed into a bright and dreamy home.

Athena's talents are not limited to interior design, as she is also a skilled visionary in the kitchen. She creates spaces from which hospitality naturally flows, and then she lives, cooks, and entertains from these places in an organic and seamless way: form feeds function. A believer in cooking with the season, Athena buys food for her family at farmers' markets or directly from farms themselves. Family and friends envy her affinity for herbs, which she uses in virtually every dish that comes out of her kitchen. Her family claims she is always chopping herbs, which seems to be a fitting pastime for someone with a meticulously cultivated herb garden in her backyard.

When she is not cooking or renovating another home, Athena runs a blog called *EyeSwoon*, which gathers all the beautiful and inspiring places and foods that catch her aesthetic attention. It is a virtual space for the rest of the world to catch a glimpse of what Athena sees and shapes. Since pulling up a seat at her reclaimed pine kitchen island is not an option for most, this platform brings her beauty directly into our own living rooms, our own kitchens. If we are lucky, we will all be able to add a bit more beauty—of the food and decor variety—into our own lives. ◆

Cedar-Plank-Grilled Halibut with Herb Pesto Salad

ATHENA: *This halibut was inspired by a similar dish I had at Little Owl in New York years ago, and it truly represents summer to me. With its clean, vibrant flavors and abundance of the season's best veggies, this dish packs a punch of flavor with fresh herbs and the brightness of lemons. It's perfect for either lunch or dinner and for guests. The cedar planks give the fish a wonderful woodsy flavor and keep the fish incredibly moist.*

FOR THE PESTO

1 cup (1 ounce/30 grams) fresh basil leaves

2 garlic cloves, peeled

Kosher salt and freshly ground black pepper

½ cup (120 milliliters) extra-virgin olive oil, plus additional as needed

Grated zest and juice of 1 lemon

FOR THE PESTO

In a food processor, pulse the basil, garlic, ½ teaspoon salt, ½ teaspoon pepper, and the ½ cup (120 milliliters) olive oil until finely chopped. Transfer the pesto to a medium bowl and stir in the lemon zest and juice. Stir in additional oil, 1 tablespoon (15 milliliters) at a time, to adjust the consistency as desired. Season with additional salt and pepper to taste.

FOR THE HALIBUT AND SALAD

Soak a cedar plank about 15 by 6 inches (38 by 15 centimeters) in cold water for 1 hour prior to using. Light a charcoal grill and allow the coals to turn ashy and white. If using a gas grill, heat to high according to the manufacturer's instructions.

Meanwhile, bring a large pot of water to a boil over high heat. Add the corn and cook just until tender, about 2 minutes, then transfer to a large plate. When the corn is cool enough to handle, scrape off the kernels with a sharp knife.

Return the water to a boil and cook the peas just until tender, 1 to 2 minutes. Transfer them to a salad bowl with a slotted spoon.

FOR THE HALIBUT AND
SALAD

4 ears corn, husked

1½ cups (4½ ounces/130 grams)
fresh or frozen peas

2 pounds (910 grams) fresh
halibut, cut into 4 fillets

2 tablespoons (30 milliliters)
extra-virgin olive oil

Salt and freshly ground black
pepper

1 bunch of frisée, rinsed and
dried

1 small red onion, thinly sliced
into half-moons

1 pint (about 12 ounces/
310 grams) cherry or grape
tomatoes, halved

Drizzle the fish with the oil and season it with salt and pepper to taste. Set aside.

Set the soaked cedar plank on the grill and heat for 2 minutes. Arrange the fillets on the plank, close the grill, and cook until they are opaque and cooked through, 8 to 10 minutes.

Meanwhile, add the frisée, onion, corn kernels, and tomatoes to the salad bowl and toss to combine. Add two-thirds of the pesto and toss once again to coat. Season with salt and pepper to taste.

Divide the salad among four plates and top each with one piece of halibut. Drizzle the remaining pesto over the fish. Serve immediately.

Notes: The pesto can also be made with a combination of herbs.

To enhance the basil flavor, add a handful of torn basil leaves to the salad.

Pictured on page 306
Serves 4

Sugar Snap Peas with Fresh Mint and Whipped Ricotta

1 pound (455 grams) fresh sugar snap peas, strings removed

¾ cup (6¾ ounces/190 grams) whole-milk ricotta

4 scallions, white and pale green parts only, thinly sliced

2 tablespoons (30 milliliters) extra-virgin olive oil

1 tablespoon (15 milliliters) fresh lemon juice

½ cup (½ ounce/15 grams) fresh mint leaves, thinly sliced

Maldon sea salt

ATHENA: *My son could eat this dish daily . . . as could the entire family. Once spring arrives, snap peas are in abundance at the farm stands and soooo fresh and yummy!*

Bring a small pot of water to a boil over medium-high heat. Fill a large bowl with equal parts ice cubes and cold water to make an ice bath.

Blanch the peas until they turn bright green, about 1 minute, then drain them and drop them into the prepared ice bath.

Meanwhile, pulse the ricotta in a food processor until it's smooth and creamy.

Drain the peas and pat them dry. Toss them in a large bowl with the scallions, olive oil, and lemon juice.

Dollop one-quarter of the whipped ricotta on each of four plates. Top the ricotta with the peas, then sprinkle them with the mint and salt. Serve immediately.

Serves 4 as an appetizer

FRANCES PALMER

{ CERAMICIST }

WESTON, CONNECTICUT

Frances Palmer is a crafter of fine pottery. She's known around the world for her artistic vessels—bowls, serving dishes, mugs, vases, and more—that are as functional as they are decorative, carrying offerings of both nourishment and joy. She knows that food is but one element in the dining experience; dishes and flowers also provide natural color and life.

Frances was a studio artist—a printmaker—and an art historian before she ever touched the potter's wheel. However, after discovering that pottery resided at the intersection of her passions—cooking, gardening, and working with her hands—she knew she had found her niche, a way to create tools that are used to bring people together over food and drink. Shaping clay is intimate work, about creating

"When our children were small, I would cook dinner and we would eat together most evenings. Now they are living on their own and they are good entertainers as well. Their friends come to them for a meal and that makes me very happy."
—FRANCES PALMER

a product that will be loved and shared by real people around real tables for years to come. The spirit behind her work speaks to the living quality of material goods. Frances understands attachment to cherished items—like her own cast-iron skillet, which has been her constant kitchen companion since her college days—that serve an exceptional purpose. Each piece becomes much greater than the sum of its substance, be it a cast-iron pan, a ceramic mug, or a trusted workhorse mixer.

Now residing in the fields of Weston, Connecticut, Frances lives a quiet and romantic life alongside her husband, Wally, and their dog and cat. The couple shares a natural affinity for early mornings and rich coffee, which they partake of together every day. Their three grown children now live on their own, cooking and entertaining just as their mother taught them. Frances has left her mark on her family, much like she leaves it on the many kitchen tables where her work lives. ◆

"I try to prepare as much of the meal from scratch as possible. Thus, I'll make the pasta or the ice cream, the cake, the salad dressing—anything that can be made versus bought, I will do. I also try to have the flowers that I grow in the vases that I make. The plates are my own as well, so I try to create a complete handmade environment. I like fresh ingredients and now have a good vegetable garden. My neighbor has chickens and there are great farmers' markets here, so I am able to find wonderful food year-round."

—FRANCES PALMER

Perfect Roast Chicken

One 3½- to 4-pound (1.6- to 1.8-kilogram) whole chicken, preferably organic

3 tablespoons (42 grams) unsalted butter

Kosher salt and freshly ground black pepper

½ lemon

½ pear

3 garlic cloves, peeled

1 small bunch of fresh herbs such as sage, rosemary, and tarragon

1½ teaspoons (0.15 ounce/ 4.5 grams) paprika

3 medium russet potatoes (about 24 ounces/680 grams), scrubbed and cut into 1½-inch (4-centimeter) pieces

2 large yellow onions, peeled and quartered

1 pound (455 grams) seasonal vegetables, peeled and cut into 1½-inch (4-centimeter) pieces

3 tablespoons (45 milliliters) olive oil

Position a rack in the center of the oven and preheat the oven to 400°F (204°C).

Wash the chicken inside and out under cold running water, then thoroughly pat it dry with paper towels. Rub the cavity with 1 tablespoon (14 grams) of the butter, ½ teaspoon salt, and ½ teaspoon pepper, then insert the lemon, pear, garlic, and herbs.

Combine 1 teaspoon (6 grams) salt, ½ teaspoon pepper, and the paprika in a small bowl and rub the mixture all over the chicken. Tuck the wings behind the chicken. Tie the drumsticks together with kitchen twine. Arrange the chicken breast side up in a 12-inch (30-centimeter) seasoned cast-iron skillet. Cut the remaining 2 tablespoons (28 grams) butter into small pieces and scatter them over the chicken.

Arrange the potatoes, onions, and vegetables around the chicken. Drizzle the olive oil over the vegetables and season them with salt and pepper.

Roast the chicken for 1½ to 2 hours or until a thermometer inserted in the breast registers 150°F (66°C). Transfer the chicken to a carving board and allow to rest for 10 to 15 minutes prior to carving.

Meanwhile, skim off the excess fat from the skillet and serve the chicken and vegetables together with the pan juices.

Notes: An apple or pitted peach half can be added to the chicken cavity instead of the pear.

The russet potatoes may be replaced with sweet potatoes.

Save all leftover bones and vegetables for a beautiful stock.

Serves 4

Butterscotch Pudding

6 large egg yolks, at room
temperature

2 cups (480 milliliters) heavy
cream

1 cup (240 milliliters) whole
milk

¼ cup (2 ounces/60 grams)
firmly packed dark brown sugar

½ cup (3½ ounces/100 grams)
granulated sugar

¼ cup (60 milliliters) water

1 teaspoon (5 milliliters) vanilla
extract

½ teaspoon kosher salt

Whipped cream, for serving
(optional)

Position a rack in the center of the oven and preheat the oven to 300°F (149°C). Place a clean dish towel in the bottom of a roasting pan.

In a large bowl, whisk the egg yolks until smooth; set aside.

In a medium heavy saucepan, bring the cream, milk, and brown sugar to a simmer over medium-high heat, stirring until the sugar is completely dissolved. Remove the pan from the heat and cover to keep warm.

In a large heavy saucepan, bring the granulated sugar and water to a simmer over medium-high heat, stirring until the sugar is completely dissolved. Increase the heat to high and boil, swirling the pan occasionally, until the mixture turns dark amber and just begins to smoke, 5 to 7 minutes. Immediately pour in the cream mixture in a slow steady stream. Be careful—the mixture will bubble and sputter aggressively (which is why a large pan is important; it will overflow in a pan with low sides). Once the bubbling and sputtering have subsided, stir the mixture over medium heat until smooth.

Wrap a damp towel around the base of the egg yolk bowl to keep it steady. In a very slow, steady stream, whisk in the caramel mixture. Stir in the vanilla and salt. Strain the mixture into a large bowl and divide it among six 6-ounce (180 milliliter) ramekins or ovenproof teacups. (Alternatively, this can be made in a 2-quart/1.89-liter baking dish; increase the baking time to 2 hours.)

Set the ramekins in the prepared roasting pan and place it in the oven. Pour enough hot water into the pan to reach about halfway up the sides of the ramekins. Cover the roasting pan with foil and bake until the puddings tremble slightly in the center when shaken gently, about 1 hour. Transfer the roasting pan to a rack, remove the foil, and cool the puddings completely in the water.

Refrigerate the puddings until well chilled, at least 2 hours and for up to a day. Serve with whipped cream if desired. The pudding may be prepared a day in advance and kept in the refrigerator.

Serves 6

SARA & HUGH FORTE

{ FOOD WRITER/RECIPE DEVELOPER
AND PHOTOGRAPHER }
DANA POINT, CALIFORNIA

The mornings are particularly sweet times in the home of Sara and
Hugh Forte, where the two start their days serving each other—Sara
brings her baked goods to the table, Hugh his pour-over coffee. A
commitment to making this meal together every morning is a way
for these unabashed big-breakfast enthusiasts to bring themselves a
moment of stillness before life's distractions pull them away.

The creators of the popular food blog *Sprouted Kitchen*, Sara and
Hugh make delicious whole foods in their own sprouted kitchen in
Southern California. They started the blog as a hobby, based on Sara's
love of food and Hugh's eye behind the camera. Their side project
quickly transformed into a community of people gathered around
their site eager to learn and have a dialogue about the role of whole
foods in their lives. Hugh, a professional photographer, continues to
document the process and products with astute artistry, creating an
engaging visual experience.

The pair has also published a cookbook under the same name,
which was a wild success across the blogging and cooking world at
large. Staying true to their roots, both literally and figuratively, Sara
and Hugh have maintained a simple life, focused on rich hospitality.
One of the primary goals for their marriage was to create a home in
which people would feel welcome. They decided that a life of food,
warmth, and open doors would be their way to care for friends and
family—and so it is. ◆

Chocolate Chip–Banana Pancakes

1 large egg

1 overripe banana, mashed

½ cup (120 milliliters) whole milk or nondairy milk

2 tablespoons (30 milliliters) fresh lemon or orange juice

1 tablespoon (½ ounce/ 14 grams) unsalted butter, melted, plus additional for greasing the griddle

1 teaspoon (5 milliliters) vanilla extract

½ cup (2½ ounces/70 grams) oat, all-purpose, or whole wheat pastry flour

½ cup (2 ounces/60 grams) almond meal

1½ tablespoons (¾ ounce/ 20 grams) muscovado or packed dark brown sugar

1 tablespoon (¼ ounce/7 grams) flax meal

1 teaspoon (0.1 ounce/3 grams) baking powder

1 teaspoon (0.1 ounce/3 grams) ground cinnamon

¼ cup (3 ounces/90 grams) bittersweet or semisweet chocolate chips, chopped (optional)

Maple syrup, for serving

SARA: *The chocolate chips make these pancakes more indulgent, while leaving them out still offers a nice spiced banana pancake. Let your mood guide you—the recipe is fine either way.*

Whisk the egg in a medium bowl until well beaten, then whisk in the banana, milk, lemon juice, melted butter, and vanilla and mix until well combined.

Whisk the flour, almond meal, sugar, flax meal, baking powder, and cinnamon together in a large bowl. Stir the banana mixture into the flour mixture just until combined. Allow the batter to sit at room temperature for 8 to 10 minutes, then stir in the chocolate chips, if using.

Heat a griddle over medium-low heat. Brush the griddle with butter and pour about ¼ cup (60 milliliters) of the batter onto it. Cook for 3 to 4 minutes or until the edges are set and the surface is bubbly. Flip the pancake with a spatula and cook for 2 minutes. Transfer to a plate and repeat with additional butter and the remaining batter.

Serve immediately with maple syrup.

Pictured on page 322
Makes about twelve 4-inch (10-centimeter) pancakes

Sautéed Leeks and Scrambled Eggs

2 tablespoons (1 ounce/
28 grams) unsalted butter

4 leeks, white and pale green
parts only, thinly sliced

Sea salt and freshly ground
black pepper

1 tablespoon (0.1 ounce/
3 grams) fresh thyme leaves

5 large eggs, at room
temperature

2 tablespoons (30 milliliters)
whole milk or heavy cream

Heat 1½ tablespoons (21 grams) of the butter in a large skillet over medium-high heat. Add the leeks, season with salt, and cook, stirring, for about 10 minutes or until they begin to brown. Remove the skillet from the heat, stir in 2 teaspoons of the thyme, and season with pepper. Cover and reserve.

Whisk the eggs, ½ teaspoon salt, and the milk together in a medium bowl until well blended. Melt the remaining 1½ teaspoons (7 grams) butter in a large nonstick skillet over medium heat. Add the eggs and allow them to sit for 1 to 2 minutes or until they begin to set. Gently push the eggs from one edge of the skillet to the other with a heatproof rubber spatula, allowing the uncooked eggs to spill into the cleared surface of the skillet. Repeat this procedure until the eggs are almost completely set or cooked to desired doneness, 4 minutes or more.

Transfer the eggs to two plates, season with salt, and sprinkle with the remaining 1 teaspoon thyme. Serve alongside the sautéed leeks.

Pictured on page 322
Serves 2

SHAUNA ALTERIO & STEPHEN LOIDOLT

{ DESIGNERS/HABERDASHERS }

PHILADELPHIA, PENNSYLVANIA

Shauna Alterio and Stephen Loidolt seem to endlessly heap projects onto their lives. Never ones to back down from creative challenges, this talented couple has produced countless beautiful works. Their blog, *Something's Hiding in Here*, has brought them into America's living rooms, while their necktie and bow tie line, Forage, has brought updated haberdashery to men at soirées, at work, and at wedding parties. As if these two projects weren't enough, they also run a small stationery shop with products reminiscent of antique treasures found in your grandmother's dusty attic. Their collective imagination seems perpetual: one idea takes life, moves forward, and gives birth to yet another.

What originally started as an enterprise in making Christmas gifts for their close friends soon became a business venture. Nowadays, this warm, dynamic couple never seems to stop. When they aren't blogging, sewing ties, or letterpressing stationery, they are still on the move—collaborating on pop-up shops, design shows, and more. They manage all this while maintaining a loving and inspired marriage, including enjoying lazy meals on the weekends.

Over the past few years, Stephen and Shauna have found a particular affinity for that languorous meal that floats between the late morning hours and the early afternoon—brunch. It was fitting that when we visited they made us brunch, homey foods that somehow both wake and calm the spirit. In their loft, which moves seamlessly from kitchen to library to work space to bedroom, Stephen and Shauna move in true rhythm together. It makes sense that their creative products hint at heritage, family, and connectedness, because Stephen and Shauna unfailingly reflect these virtues. ◆

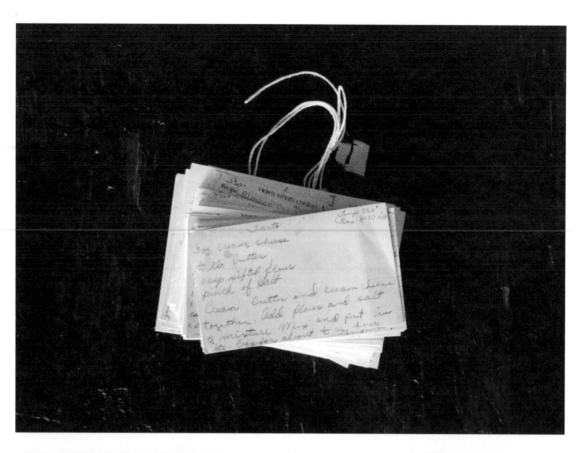

Shortcakes with Fresh Berries and Whipped Cream

SHAUNA: *I've always been obsessed with berries of all types. I try to find a way to work them into as many meals as I can. For the past thirteen years, these shortcakes have been one of our family dishes, especially during the summer, when berries are abundant and local farms allow you to come pick your own.*

FOR THE SHORTCAKES

Position a rack in the center of the oven and preheat the oven to 350°F (177°C). Line a baking sheet with parchment paper.

Whisk the flour, 2 tablespoons (25 grams) sugar, baking powder, and cream of tartar in a large bowl. Using two knives, cut the butter into the flour mixture until it resembles small peas. Stir in the cream and egg.

Quickly combine the dough with your hands. Lightly flour a clean, dry work surface. Turn the dough out and knead it for about 2 minutes or just until combined.

Drop 6 large spoonfuls of the dough onto the prepared baking sheet, spacing them about 1 inch (2.5 centimeters) apart. Brush the tops with the melted butter and sprinkle them with sugar.

Bake the shortcakes for about 20 minutes or until golden. Transfer the sheet to a rack and cool for about 10 minutes.

FOR THE WHIPPED CREAM AND ASSEMBLY

Whisk the cream, confectioners' sugar, and vanilla in a large bowl for 2 to 3 minutes or until the mixture holds soft peaks.

Serve the shortcakes warm with whipped cream and fresh berries.

Serves 6

GRACE WILLIAMS

{ GARDENER/RETIRED NURSE }
LETHBRIDGE, ALBERTA, CANADA

Grace Williams, my grandmother, spends her days researching family genealogy, making meals, and tending to her garden while also maintaining a rigorous (and dramatic!) schedule of daytime soap operas. This idyllic life has followed her career as a nurse, a profession of diligence and compassion. Her days are now filled with making preserves and drying fruit leathers, using produce straight from her bountiful garden. Growing up, my cousins and I would make games out of sifting through Grandma's jars of sweet fruit jams and digging through her storehouse of dehydrated fruits. Each of her fruit leathers was stamped with the date, so on occasion we would compete to find the oldest treat when reaching a hand into the pantry, sometimes finding pieces from decades earlier that she would claim were still in their prime. Bless her heart, they were hardly edible.

My grandmother is unmistakably from another generation, in all of the best ways. She is content sharing homemade chocolates at Christmas and frozen boxes of raspberries in the summer as gifts year after year. She cooks often, worrying little about making things extravagant or new, relying instead on trusted meals that are sure to keep herself, the family, and friends at ease. She understands simple gestures and upholds time-honored courtesies like sending handwritten notes. (She even insisted on mailing her handwritten recipe for this collection.) She still writes letters to her scattered friends and family members on a weekly basis, a simple example of the kindness she extends to caring for those in her life.

A good day would be one spent with Grandma Grace, sitting with her as she organizes her collection of family photos, following her through the garden, picking through her jams, and poking fun at her fossilized fruit leather. Being with Grandma Grace is an exercise in humility, because for her, the simple acts of canning, gardening, and making those annual Christmas chocolates are not just hobbies—they are her acts of love.

Grace's Raspberry Harvest Jam

4 cups (about 32 ounces/
900 grams) mixed fresh berries,
crushed

5¼ cups (36¾ ounces/
1 kilogram) sugar

¾ cup (175 milliliters) water

1 package pectin (1 ounce/
28 grams)

Stir the berries and sugar together in a large bowl and allow to stand for 10 minutes.

Combine the water and pectin in a small saucepan and bring to a boil over medium-high heat, stirring constantly. Boil for 1 minute, then stir the pectin mixture into the fruit mixture. Ladle the jam into sterilized jars, leaving ½ inch (1.28 centimeters) of space at the top. Cover the jars tightly and allow to set for at least 2 hours and up to 24 hours.

Transfer any jam you want to store long term to resealable plastic bags and freeze for up to 1 year.

Makes 3 pints/1.4 liters

GUS AGNANOPOULOS & JESSE JAMES

{ POET AND DESIGNER }
QUEENS, NEW YORK

Within the Jackson Heights historic district in Queens, across the street from the local church garden, live Gus Agnanopoulos and his husband, Jesse James, in a building that surrounds a block-long courtyard garden. It is here that they raise their darling daughter, Olympia, and where they have settled into the routines of family life together. Gus and Olympia welcomed us into their home with strong pour-over coffee, paired with sweet honey-and-sesame treats.

This family is inspiring, both for their intentionality and their ambition. Together, Gus and Jesse started Aesthetic Movement, a creative consultancy, design, and representation business that has grown to national acclaim over the years. Additionally, Gus is a published poet with a master of fine arts degree in writing. Both are naturally fluid and adept in the kitchen. Their life at home is purposeful, with meals eaten together as often as possible and traditions incorporated wherever they can be. The couple established a weekly movie and late-night dinner date, and on weekend mornings the routine is homemade waffles. The waffles are Olympia's favorite, and also a decade-old tradition from Jesse's family in Connecticut.

The family's eating habits and tastes represent the diverse tapestry of their backgrounds, their families of origin, and their geographies. Gus grew up with parents who cured their own olives in a closet in their home and who make and bottle their own wine. These distinctly Greek traditions have bestowed on him a palate that highly favors fine wine, olive oil, and honey. It was no wonder, then, that Gus prepared us bright green, sesame-seasoned broccoli, drizzled with a rich, flavorful olive oil.

The food on the table set before us was fragrant and fresh, and the aesthetic was highly personal, represented by the collected and meaningful objects from Gus's and Jesse's lives. The flatware, the serving dishes, the linen tea towels—all carried stories as the couple laid the table for our meal. Our time spent at this charming home in Queens was an experience both visual and physical, sprung from heritage and sustained by a committed family. •

"I always try to work with what is in our cupboards and refrigerator, and I adjust recipes accordingly. I tend to cook simple meals; partly because I think the flavor is already in the food, and partly because our daughter, Olympia, is young and needs to get to sleep early. To enhance flavors I stick to good salt, black pepper, olive oil, Parmigiano-Reggiano, sometimes honey, and fresh herbs, which I always have hanging in our kitchen."

—GUS AGNANOPOULOS

Pastelli

1 cup (5 ounces/140 grams) sesame seeds

⅓ cup (1.7 ounces/50 grams) raw pistachios or almonds, coarsely chopped

1½ tablespoons (1.1 ounces/ 32 grams) honey

Toast the sesame seeds in a medium skillet over medium heat, stirring constantly, until light golden, about 5 minutes. Stir in the nuts and cook for 1 minute longer. Add the honey and stir until the sesame seeds and nuts are coated evenly.

Spoon the mixture onto a clean, dry surface and use the back of the spoon to pat the pastelli into an 8-inch (20-centimeter) square. Wet your hands in cold water (it helps to have a small bowl of it nearby) and smooth out the surface and edges. Alternatively, use a rolling pin.

Cool the pastelli for 15 minutes, then cut it into 16 squares. Serve. Store any leftover pastelli between layers of wax paper in an airtight container.

Note: A cold surface, such as marble or a marble pastry board, is the ideal surface for making pastelli.

Makes 16 squares

THANK YOU

To Amanda Jane Jones for her creative eye, her classic art direction, and her lead on the design of this book. Thanks for being such an easygoing, humble, and enthusiastic creative partner on projects over the past two years.

To Parker Fitzgerald and Leo Patrone for their talent behind the camera, for their dedication to film, and for welcoming my feedback and styling on these shoots.

To Rebecca Parker Payne for lending her hand and pen to capture meals and moments we shared with our friends in their homes, and for her patience traveling with me for many of these interviews.

To María del Mar Sacasa for her late nights spent editing and testing recipes, trips to the market, and even last-minute tests in unfamiliar kitchens while she was traveling.

Special thanks to Nathalie Schwer, Silvana de Soissons, Rosa Park, and Nicolee Drake for donating so many hours to coordinate our visits to their home cities.

To my wife, Katie, and closest friends, Doug and Paige Bischoff, for holding down the *Kinfolk* fort while I was away and to Julie Pointer for her help editing and collecting interviews.

To our editor, Lia Ronnen, for her confidence in our team, her experience with publishing, her willingness to share tips of the trade, and her frank feedback when my ideas were both helpful and horrible. Also at Artisan, thanks to Ann Bramson, Sibylle Kazeroid, Bridget Heiking, Michelle Ishay-Cohen, Kara Strubel, Nancy Murray, Trent Duffy, and Allison McGeehon.

To our agent, Susie Finesman, for her early and ongoing encouragement.

Lastly, thanks to the friends we have included in these profiles for their warm welcome and hospitality. Thanks for opening their doors, sharing their kitchens, and passing along their favorite recipes, even when that required some gentle prying from their protective hands. ◆

INDEX